W9-AVO-590

The Coach Approach

Success Strategies **From The Locker Room To The Board Room**

John Brubaker

Be Your Best!!

Coach Bru .com
JOHN BRUBAKER

John Brubaker
The Coach Approach:
Success Strategies from the Locker Room to the Board Room

© 2012 by John Brubaker
All rights reserved. No part of this book may be reproduced or transmitted in any form or by any means, electronic or mechanical, including photocopying, recording, or by any information storage and retrieval system, without express written permission from the author, except for the inclusion of brief quotations in critical articles or a review.

Requests for permission should be made in writing to:

John Brubaker
The Sport of Business, LLC
51 Waters Edge Dr.
Lewiston, ME. 04240

Edited by: Ann Whetstone and Paula Keeney
Cover and interior design: Doris Bruey

Library of Congress Control Number: 2012902033
ISBN 978-0-9850671-0-6

Printed in the United States of America

Endorsements

"If you're serious about taking your performance to the next level and building a championship caliber team, then invest in your people and buy this book."
Gary Goldberg
Chief Executive Officer
Clean Brands LLC

"John's approach to performance using the language and metaphor of sports, hits the mark! His focus on passion, attitude and motivation makes for not only an inspiring and fun read, but lays the foundation for doing the hard work necessary for success in any endeavor. I look forward to having *The Coach Approach* on my bookshelf."
Sue Clay DeMarco
Director of Organizational Development, Exeter Hospital,
Exeter, New Hampshire

"In *The Coach Approach*, Coach Bru shares compelling, personal leadership lessons on what it takes to lead and perform at a high level. If you want to bring about game changing performance from your team members get *The Coach Approach*. You'll be glad you did."
Dave Haglund,
Commissioner, Great Northwest Athletic Conference,
Spokane, Washington

"John Brubaker's book is mission critical for leaders seeking to enhance their own performance and that of their team. *The Coach Approach* provides brilliant insights into how leaders can help their teams get to the next level."

Terry Gobble
Director of Business Development
Primo Water Corporation
Winston Salem, North Carolina

"I have known John since 1997, as both a coach and a consultant. I can tell you John understands how to turn a group into a high performing team because he understands people. His approach is one that teaches fundamental principles, which when applied will create a culture of personal excellence for your employees and organization."

Anthony Fallacaro, Director of Athletics
Post University
Waterbury, Connecticut

"*The Coach Approach* is a fantastic combination of education, motivation, and inspiration for leaders in any industry. John Brubaker writes in a clear, engaging, and highly accessible style that is a true pleasure to read. Even someone who considers himself a non-reader will enjoy this book, as it feels more like you are listening to a very bright friend and mentor sharing his insights with you over a cup of coffee."

David Lee
Principal
HumanNatureAtWork.com

"A lot of leaders in business and education have developed their leadership and teambuilding skills through participation in athletics. *The Coach Approach* gives readers a fascinating look at the many parallels between coaching a sports team at the highest level, and leading an organization in the business world. Take the lessons Coach Bru shares to heart."

Daniel Cardone, Director of Athletics
North Hills School District, Pennsylvania

Dedication

This book is dedicated to the many coaches and teammates I've played with throughout my life. I am the product of so many people and experiences. Growing up my coaches and family have been my role models and mentors. That said, to my coaches, thank you for treating me like family. To my parents, Thomas and Geraldine, thank you for coaching this rookie and teaching him the rules of the game of life.

To the coaches and mentors in my professional life— Dr. Amy Wood, Barbara Babkirk, David Lee, Dick Babb, and Pastor Rich Cullen—thank you for your guidance in serving as my personal board of directors. Your unwavering support, feedback, and insight have helped push me to maximize my potential. To my editorial team, Paula Keeney and Ann Whetstone at Communications Ink, I appreciate your wisdom and insight more than you know.

To my wife, Bethany, my best friend and the most influential person in my life, you are the best teammate I have ever known. Thank you for keeping me centered and grounded. To my children, Meredith and Julia, thank you for being the ultimate life coaches. Everyday I learn more from you about perseverance and the human spirit than any professor or textbook could ever teach.

In gratitude, I am donating a portion of the proceeds from this book to the Deaf Children's Literacy Project.

Acknowledgements

Coach John Wooden once said, "It takes ten hands to make a basket." I would add it takes many minds to make a book. I owe a debt of gratitude to many people. Thanks to Jon Gordon, best-selling author, world-class speaker, and even better mentor and person! Your counsel, inspiration, and insights have been priceless.

Thanks also to my coaches for sharing their wisdom and so bringing out the best in me as a student-athlete and person. Please know the lessons you've shared continue to be executed daily. A special thank-you goes out to the many assistant coaches I have had on my staff over the years. I have learned as much from you as you have from me.

Great players make for great coaches as the saying goes. With that in mind, I cannot thank enough the hundreds of student-athletes I've had the honor and privilege of mentoring over the years. You are outstanding athletes but more importantly, world-class people.

Lastly, this book would not be the same without the wisdom of the coaches, athletes, and CEOs referenced in these pages.

The Coach Approach represents the perfect bridge between my two professional careers: from coach/educator to consultant. Prior to returning to the world of consulting, I spent 12 wonderful years in the leadership and teambuilding business as a college lacrosse coach.

Coaching at a small college prepared me better for my current role than I ever imagined. It is the ultimate laboratory for creating a culture of excellence. Coaches are responsible for teaching, recruiting, budgeting, community/media relations, strategy, accountability, NCAA compliance, team culture, chemistry, leadership development, succession planning, mentoring, and building an environment of high performance.

Every day is a performance review; most days are an exercise in handling pressure; and some are a study in crisis management.

It was through writing this book that I came to the realization that I never really left coaching as a career. The principles I have used to build successful lacrosse teams are the very same ones on which great organizations are built. I have not changed; rather my "recruits" and team members have changed.

Thank you for reading *The Coach Approach*. Enjoy your journey and remember that little things win big games.

Table of Contents

Full Circle

It has often been said that art imitates life and that sport is a microcosm of society. I would add that coaching imitates consulting and vice versa.

My career has come full circle. My approach to coaching was strongly influenced and shaped not only by my experience as a collegiate athlete and my coaching mentors but also, perhaps even more, by consulting practices. During graduate school I worked in the field of performance enhancement as a staff consultant for Human Resource Associates Inc. I performed job analysis and re-design for several manufacturing organizations. Through this experience I was able to take theories about the functioning of individual performance on teams from concept to reality. It was also at this time that I was first introduced to the Kolb and Frohman model of organizational development. This model spoke to the athlete and coach in me and has impacted my career since.

The personal coaching philosophy I have followed since day one virtually mirrors the stages of organization and development that Kolb and Frohman developed. I have inserted coaching terms within their description of these stages to better illustrate the parallels.

- *Scouting:* Data collection to get a feel for the client (team, recruit, or opponent).

- *Diagnosis:* Get a clear picture of the client (team, recruit, or opponent) strengths, weaknesses, attitudes, problems, and overall operations.

- *Planning:* Planning interventions (practice plan, game plan, strategy) to apply, where, and how.

- *Action:* The motivation step, beginning the process of change with a client (team, student-athlete).

- *Evaluation:* Monitoring and assessing the intervention strategy (game plan). Associated costs and benefits upon completion.

What can business leaders learn from coaches? There are many parallels and transferable skills from the athletic arena to the sport of business. Business organizations and athletic teams both consist of individuals brought together to work toward a common goal. The collective efforts of these teams are far greater than anything the individuals could ever dream of achieving alone.

Sport truly is a metaphor for life. I will be sharing with you the many ways my methods of leading a college lacrosse program are analogous to your leading an organization. The best way to utilize *The Coach Approach* as a resource is to think of yourself as the head coach of your organization, department, or work team. I will be addressing mission critical areas of team success such as recruitment, game planning, communication, sportsmanship, success, attitude, mental toughness, and leadership.

You don't have to have been an athlete or coach to apply the strategies you will read about. You can use them to create your own playbook to enhance your skills, knowledge, and abilities and so advance further in your career.

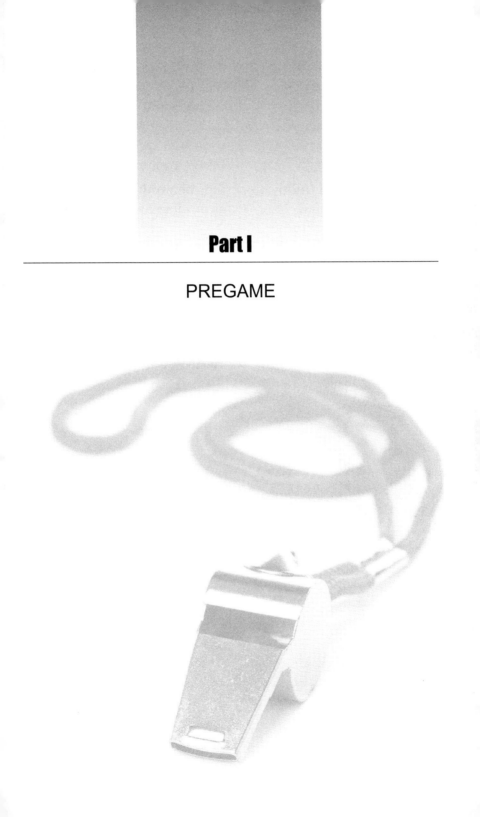

Part I

PREGAME

Scouting Report

In theory there is no difference between theory and practice; in practice there is.

Yogi Berra, Baseball player and great
American philosopher

Immediately after our NCAA Final Four loss in 2002, a newspaper reporter at the postgame press conference asked my players how we managed to play such a close game against the five-time defending conference champion Limestone College. Don't get me wrong, the loss was heartbreaking but I loved my players' responses. It spoke to what was the cornerstone of our program, preparation. Their responses were all variations on a theme. "We were well prepared," "We had them so well scouted that we could anticipate what they were going to do before they did it," "We knew their tendencies so well one of their players commented to me that it seemed like we were listening in on their huddles during time outs," "We studied their plays on video, had a solid game plan, and practiced that game plan every day leading up to today."

In short, those answers and dogged determination are precisely what kept us in that game. We knew our opponents as well if not better than they knew themselves. At the same time, we knew exactly who we were and who we weren't. When you are outmanned, a good scouting report and superior preparation can level the playing field for you, ensuring you're not outmatched.

This scouting report is the how-to of using *The Coach Approach* as a resource to enhance your performance. One of the most important aspects of game preparation for any team is the scouting report. Through a detailed scouting report, you can gain greater insight into the opposition's strengths and potential weaknesses. By watching an opponent's previous games you can identify matchups that can be exploited to gain a competitive advantage on game day. Even more important than the scouting report we prepared on the opposition was the self-scout performed by coaches and mentors I invited to our practices and shared our game films. These trusted colleagues were the sports equivalent of retaining a consultant to analyze the performance of my business team.

The great American philosopher (and baseball legend) Yogi Berra once very eloquently said, *"In theory there is no difference between theory and practice; in practice there is."* This is where *The Coach Approach* brings clarity to the picture. It bridges the gap between theory and practice. In most organizations and teams there is an enormous gap between theory and the execution of the theory. In this book you will find straightforward strategies you can employ both individually and in teams. Focus on strategically implementing them one at a time, and you will be on your way to building a championship-caliber game plan for success. These are not theoretical or pie-in-the-sky approaches but rather hands-on, real-life examples in action that you can replicate. These strategies have brought about game-changing results for my teams and clients over the years. As a result, I am confident they will do the same for you.

Just as a scouting report helps better prepare you for game day, this book will better prepare you to take your game to the next level. Add to these strategies or pare them down to meet the unique needs of your team and organization. Designate time to reflect on and complete the Coaching Points at the end of each chapter. They are a tool for analysis, focus, and better self-awareness. They are in essence your detailed self-scout.

Much like a lacrosse game and a fiscal year, the book is divided into quarters. The first quarter is designed to introduce you to the parallels between sport and business. The second quarter concentrates on individual performance enhancement in the workplace and the power of focus. The second half of the book delves into team performance strategies in the third quarter and teaches you what the best in any field do that makes them so much more successful than the rest in the fourth quarter.

At various points in *The Coach Approach*, you will also find Time Outs. These provide you with additional tips, strategies, and expanded Coaching Points to help you bring about game-changing performance. Consider these Coaching Points a pregame warm-up.

Coaching Points

- What do you think you would read in a scouting report written about yourself? Strengths? Weaknesses? Tendencies? Communication style?

- How would you prefer it to read?

- What would a scouting report on your organization read like? Strengths? Weaknesses? Who are the go-to guys? What is the number-one core strength of the team? Brand image? Market share?

- How would you prefer this to read?

- After reading the answers to the questions above, would you want to compete against your team?

Part II

FIRST QUARTER

Chapter 1

Overtime Victory

For me, winning isn't something that happens suddenly.
Winning is something that builds mentally every day that you work
toward your goal and every night that you dream.
Emmitt Smith, Hall of Fame NFL running back

*T**he Coach Approach* is a process of self-discovery. I utilize the mantra "Overtime Victory" with the organizations and executives I coach. It is used as a trigger word to remind them there is no such thing as an overnight success. The best make it look easy. Superstar athletes and musicians perform so seemingly effortlessly that the public tends to think they were simply born with a gift. The reality is their success was born of years of resilience and hard work before anyone was watching. You, too, can do the same. Management gurus Malcolm Gladwell and Jim Collins echo my Overtime Victory sentiment with their theories that it takes at least 10 years or 10,000 hours of practicing a skill to become an expert.

Particularly in this instant, on-demand society we live in, patience is becoming an endangered species. The younger generation of athletes and employees find it extremely hard to maintain their patience when they are not seeing their efforts yield immediate results. This is why sport is such a great teacher of business. It is a true meritocracy yet it is unforgiving. It is an ever-changing environment that requires you to be

9

nimble yet consistent. It is complex yet requires you to focus on fundamentals. In order to survive and thrive, you must be patient. Patience is the cornerstone of longevity. Little things win big games, in sports and in business. The key to keeping your attitude up in downtimes is to seek and celebrate small successes each day. I teach my athletes that practice is like a daily deposit in the bank. When game day arrives, there are then "ample funds" to draw from for success. Business professionals are no different than athletes in this regard. They need the same coaching because daily deposits of success accrue interest over time and will pay dividends later. Invest in your success daily to orchestrate your own personal overtime victory.

Optimism is the ultimate competitive advantage in this economy, and positivity can be contagious in organizations. To develop it and spread it, organizations need a positivity process in place they can execute. Without it you are shooting in the dark or relying on luck. The way I coach people to "bank" their deposits is through the practice of micro-journaling. I provide my clients with a journal I published based on a principle I call "3 by 5". They are coached to keep the journal in a convenient location where they can micro-journal (deposit) three successes daily by 5 p.m. To help them focus on seeking out small successes during the day, the journal comes with a reminder coin to carry in their pocket. The concept is that when you hit an obstacle, you can refer back to your many deposits as a focusing tool to return to a positive mind-set for your long-term goals. To cultivate and maintain a positive attitude, you need to document positive actions, outcomes, and processes on a daily basis. The mantra is Overtime Victory.

When Tiger Woods was a ten-year-old boy, he wrote down on a 3 × 5 card that he intended to break all of Jack Nicklaus' golf records. Nicklaus agreed that Woods could do it if he stayed on the track he was on. Tiger openly admits that from early childhood he not only dreamed of becoming the world's best golfer but also set goals and applied himself to do so. By being so goal oriented and approaching his craft with laser focus, Woods was able to reach a level of success rarely imagined. The most effective way to write your goals down is to use a 3 × 5 card. For many years I have carried a goal card in my pocket, and I encourage clients to do the same. On one side write or type your goal and a deadline date. On the other side write your "why," which is driving the greater purpose of your goal. "I will achieve this because . . ." Laminate the card and read the card frequently over the course of each day to serve as a focusing tool. Goals help you focus on where you want to be, what you want to do, or who you want to become. By intentionally placing your focus there, you will begin moving in that direction. When you write your goals down, your subconscious mind begins to figure out ways to achieve these goals. Your thoughts determine your actions; your actions determine your performance; and your performance determines what you accomplish. As a result, you become that which you consistently think about and perform. Therefore it stands to reason that you must consistently focus on thinking about your goals.

In 1960 the Harvard Business School published a longitudinal study of its graduates 20 years after their graduation. It was found that the top 3 percent made as much money as the other 97 percent combined. There was only one little thing that made a big difference between these two groups. The top 3 percent consistently over the 20-year period had written down their goals, read them, and re-read them frequently. Clearly consistent day-to-day focus leads to success over time.

The cumulative effect of small successes results in a big increase in your personal productivity and profitability over time. Embracing this concept of continuous improvement can lead to performance breakthroughs for you in whatever area of your life you apply it: personally or professionally.

The concept of *The Coach Approach* is an offshoot of the law of accumulation, which in essence states that every great accomplishment in an individual's career is a result of the cumulative effects of hundreds or thousands of smaller activities, sacrifices, and achievements behind the scenes that combine to create the finished product. Celebrating your small successes puts you in a powerful frame of mind and strengthens your resolve moving forward.

Patience is mission critical in business and sports alike. To provide some perspective, the Dallas Cowboys went 0–11 their first season. It wasn't until eight years later that they won their first Super Bowl and eventually became know as "America's team." John Wooden, arguably the greatest coach of any sport, didn't win a title his first 15 years at UCLA. Once he got clarity on his coaching philosophy, vision, and principles, he was able to merge them into a long-term game plan for success and from 1963 to 1975 win 10 of the 12 NCAA basketball championships. Building a business is a constant struggle but a rewarding one. Learn to seek and celebrate small victories first while developing your team chemistry. As a leader, you need to focus on the big picture while keeping your teammates engaged, motivated, and positive about the immediate future.

Coaching Points

- Little things win big games. How can I make myself a little bit better each day? (After answering this, transfer your answer onto a goal card to carry with you.)

- Remember that success does not happen overnight. What steps can I take to be patient with the process of success?

- What are the fundamentals of my role that I must consistently focus on?

- Reflect on three successes you had today. What made them significant to you?

Chapter 2

Corporate Athletes

If football taught me anything about business, it's that you win the game one play at a time.

Fran Tarkenton, NFL quarterback

The parallels between being a successful executive and a successful athlete are staggering. To be a champion in either arena, you need to master several areas: productivity, goal-setting, motivation, mental toughness, and a champion's mind-set.

Like an athlete, an executive's life is hard hitting. Both competitors are in business for themselves, the business of training, competing, and winning. As a result they need to motivate themselves to consistently perform at a high level because 99 percent of the time there is no one there to make sure he or she is performing efficiently, making the right decisions, or maximizing available resources. Consequently it can be easy for them to become sidetracked. Their career success is completely dependent on their ability to prepare a game plan, focus, and overcome frequent adversity. It takes an extraordinary amount of determination, courage, and resilience to continue to show up at 100 percent physically and mentally in order to deliver a winning performance under pressure.

As you read this book, you will learn that I am a great believer in the power of metaphor in our lives. Metaphors are powerful vehicles that serve as excellent reminders for us. Consequently when I returned to a career in consulting, I wanted to create a symbolic daily reminder for myself that this journey, figuratively speaking, was a marathon not a sprint. I decided what better a way to do this than to literally train for a marathon. I began with a smaller goal of training for a half marathon. While the project began as a symbolic activity representing my journey in business, it concluded as so much more.

I initially decided to train for a half marathon with two purposes. First, I recognized that I needed a daily constant reminder that my professional and personal journey in life is a marathon not a sprint and should be treated as such. And for me, attaching a metaphor involving a sport where there are quantifiable measures of progress (clocks, timers, and rankings) helped me stay in a performance mind-set at work. It helped me ensure in my planning and work that I took a long term, methodical approach.

Secondly, the ability to recognize my physical gifts would remind me to be grateful and to train with the higher purpose of running for those who can't. My race was dedicated to family, friends, and colleagues whose lives have been touched by cancer, either firsthand or through a loved one. In 2001, I myself lost both my father and one of my former lacrosse players to cancer. My iPod play list was fueled with songs shared by them.

I believe we cannot only train and conduct our personal lives with a higher purpose in mind but also work for a higher purpose. Your business and your job have to be about more than making money; there must be a higher purpose to keep you motivated and fulfilled. I was also reminded through this process that the key to leading others lies first in effective self-leadership. I had to become my own client in that regard.

Regardless of the industry you work in, I believe you are your most important client.

Whether you are training for a marathon, a triathlon, or just performing daily fitness training, a byproduct of your efforts is that you grow stronger, increase your endurance, and develop greater mental clarity, focus, and resolve. What you discover along the way is that these are all key ingredients in winning your race in the sport of business as well. Physical fitness and fiscal fitness are intimately connected.

Additionally, you come to the realization that what initially appears to be hard work, when approached using the right process, is actually fun. You learn, grow, gain confidence, and realize that stepping up to a challenge fosters resilience. It is indeed a journey, and by engaging in a self-improvement process involving fitness, you come to realize the journey you are on is its own reward, and you should enjoy it.

Nothing worthwhile in this life goes exactly as you plan it. Therefore we all need to practice adapting, improvising, and overcoming barriers. Overcoming barriers, both physical and mental, is the key to running a successful race. It is also the key to running a successful organization. Consequently athletes and executives need to possess supreme confidence and self-efficacy. The business world is similar to the sports world in that you need to understand that there will be peaks and valleys of success and failure. If you are not confident in your abilities, you are in danger of going through a slump in your performance. The ability to be resilient and take on the trials and tribulations of the sport of business with a proper perspective will keep you from experiencing mental blocks and negative self-talk that can wreak havoc on both performance and your mind-set.

Like an athletic team playing an away game, in business you are often the away team (especially in sales). On the road, you will encounter hostile crowds, rejection, and stalling; and you usually learn along the way that it's often not a level playing field. These game day conditions can take a toll not only on the body but also on your psyche. The mental toughness strategies of a peak-performing athlete can go a long way toward helping the executive develop and maintain a champion's mind-set in areas such as motivation, energy management, handling mistakes and failure, and the value of performance rituals.

What is the value of one day of performance? In athletic training, it is hard to come back from missed training; you can't catch up simply by putting in extra time the next day. The sport of business is no different. Consider this, one workday is more than meets the eye when you look at it by percentages. It is 20 percent of your workweek, and two days are 10 percent of your month. If you lost two days each month to illness, lack of engagement, or mental blocks, it is equivalent to losing over a month of new business development annually.

The ability to focus under pressure is critical because it is often the case that several years of investment end up riding on one key play, meeting, or performance. Clients and audiences often ask me what to focus on and how to do it. My simple answer is focus on the controllables.

The first step is to identify the controllables in your role. I emphasized to my team that we only compete against two things: the game itself and ultimately ourselves. If we are competing against the opponent, the officials, the weather, the field conditions, or the crowd, we are focusing on uncontrollables. No matter how hard you try, you cannot control any of those aspects of the game. By channeling any of your energy in those directions, you are wasting your energy. This waste of energy directly contributes to a loss of focus and will significantly impair your performance.

What are the controllables in the sport of business? The easiest place to start is by identifying and ruling out the uncontrollables so you don't unnecessarily channel energy there. Take, for example, the role of sales professionals. Sales professionals do not control the economic climate, the prospect's budget, competing brands, or sales representatives from rival companies. They do, however, control their attitude, effort, and the specific sales process they follow on a daily basis. I have found it helpful to carry a list of my controllables with me in my pocket on a laminated card. Each time I reach into my pocket for my keys or some change, finding the card there serves as a frequent reminder for me to keep my focus on the right things. You may want to do the same thing. Some of my clients have created a card, others have written their controllables on their mirror and on their computer's screen saver. Take a few moments and reflect on the controllables vs. uncontrollables in your role or in your business.

Coaching Points

- List the top three uncontrollables in your business.

- List the most important controllables specific to your role.

- Make a contract with yourself to focus only on the controllables. Accept things you cannot control as they are.

17

Chapter 3

Board of Directors

Find people who have built their lives on a solid foundation, and humble yourself to learn from them. I've never known a successful athlete, business person, or anyone else who has made an impact on the world who didn't stand on the shoulders of other great men and women.

Drew Brees, NFL quarterback and MVP of Super Bowl XLIV

My "second career" as performance consultant, author, and speaker began with a process of self-discovery and exploration. As a college coach, I was accustomed to having the resources of what I called "the team behind our team"—those specialists and coaches who were a support network for our lacrosse program. The team behind the team of a college athletic program typically consists of the team physician, athletic trainer, strength and conditioning coach, nutritionist, academic advisor, tutors, sports psychologist, sports information/media relations director, NCAA compliance officer, and team chaplain, to name just a few.

Without the support and expertise of these key personnel, our teams wouldn't have enjoyed the success we did, and our players couldn't have maximized their academic and athletic potential. In order to maximize my potential, I felt I needed to develop a team behind my new team. I wanted to create a support network, accountability partners, and an unbiased third party to serve as a sounding board. Once I clearly defined my niches, I created an informal board of directors to which I reported monthly. I got this idea from reading about President Andrew Jackson, who had a trusted pack of advisors, most of whom were outside his group of official advisors. He relied on this group as a source of assistance, advice, and support.

In today's workplace of restructurings, downsizing, "rightsizing," and layoffs, having only a mentor is not stable enough nor in my opinion broad enough support. Instead, recruit a team behind your team, a diverse collection of experts to provide you with specialized feedback and advice. Every team has role players who contribute to its success. These players possess a unique talent that allows them to perform a specific task better than anyone else, thus enabling the team to reach new heights. Your board should be no different.

Based on the composition of my board, here is a list of prospective specialists you may want to recruit: attorney, business or life coach, professional peer (not friend), public relations/ marketing specialist, social media expert, academician or professor in your field, financial expert, I.T./Web expert, and spiritual advisor (if so inclined). A professional peer is particularly important as she or he will be familiar with the nuances and context of your work environment in a way others on your board may not.

An additional benefit of having a personal board of directors is that as your career path accelerates or perhaps changes, you can add to or subtract from the board to best accommodate your professional and personal needs. Consequently I recommend communicating to your board that their role is flexible and the complexion of the group may change over time. No single mentor could possibly provide you the specialized quality expertise in the way this team of expert advisors can.

I believe everyone needs a board of directors to answer questions, mentor you, help you plan, and ensure you maximize your potential in life. I sought people with depth and breadth, of diverse backgrounds and professional expertise. Having this diversity of thought can provide you with insight into blind spots. Having big picture thinkers, detail-oriented people, as well as risk takers adds an additional dimension to your board make-up. The most critical added dimension I wanted was a touch of grey—as in grey hair—several retired people with a wealth of life experience, perspective, and wisdom. Who better to counsel you than someone who has already successfully navigated the road you are traveling down?

Having a team of coaches is important in the process of self-discovery. Coaches help you discover the hidden strengths you possess and expose the weaknesses you can improve upon. Working with a board of directors or coaches enhances your ability for self-reflection because it helps you see yourself through a different lens. Typically these people will not seek you out, rather you need to locate them, and then take the initiative to nurture and maintain the relationship.

I ask the following of my board:

- Accept the coffee or lunch I buy when we meet.

- Be constructively critical and as tough on me as you feel is in my best interest.

- Be a good listener and have no fear telling me exactly what is on your mind.

Challenge me. Don't be afraid to tell me what I don't want to hear.

Having a team of mentors is only half the equation. To understand and maximize the value of the relationship, I believe one also needs to also serve as a mentor. Find an environment or organization where you can "practice" mentoring and serving others. Select an environment that parallels the work in your life and can augment or compliment your professional role as a leader. Serving as a volunteer at the Boys and Girls Club, coaching little league, and volunteering at a local nonprofit are excellent ways to learn the art of mentoring. By doing so you not only contribute to the greater good, you maximize the value of your role as mentee. I selected staying involved in coaching as a prep school lacrosse coach and serving as a volunteer board member of a nonprofit for deaf education.

In my coaching career, I noticed the biggest improvement in my players' ability to think the game and best perform their roles came when they gained a greater respect and appreciation for the roles of others involved in the game. Their understanding came through volunteer coaching in the local elementary schools and officiating youth lacrosse on off days. My placing them in this parallel environment, or "different lens," demonstrated to them the unique challenges associated with coaching and officiating, and provided them with a better understanding and appreciation of the leader's role in their growth. The student should always become the teacher from time to time.

I am a big believer in being a student of the game, whatever the game may be. This is why my players always were required to take notes during team meetings and given daily planners for time management, books to read, as well as other lacrosse, conditioning, and motivation related articles. My belief is that by becoming a student of the game, you are doing more than just playing the game. You are studying it, immersing yourself in it, and consequently boosting your lacrosse IQ. This would be one of our competitive edges over opponents who just play the game. By really *learning* the game, players have the ability to function more autonomously and figure out situations on the field themselves.

I have always wished that there were no timeouts allowed in sports and no halftime locker room meetings. If that were the case, you would be able to see which coach best taught his team in practice as well as who was a student of the game and who wasn't. Imagine the same in business, with mentoring and daily training designed to help every member and the team as a whole function successfully when it mattered most, independent of the leader. Productivity and results could soar to new heights.

Leadership expert John Maxwell is quoted as saying, "A dream without a team is a nightmare." What are you doing to promote workplace mentoring and boost the I.Q. of your team in the sport of business? Lunch and learns, continuing education, professional development seminars, and in-house training? Or are you just playing the game?

Coaching Points

- Who will you recruit to serve on your board? And how will each of them help you define, find, and utilize your talents?

- What will be your rules of engagement?

- Before you begin, ask yourself if you are capable of being brutally honest with yourself and willing to allow your board to be the same with you.

- What parallel environments will you utilize for your team in the workplace?

Chapter 4

High Five: The Science Behind It and How to Make It Work at Work

Trust is like the air we breathe.
When it's present, nobody really notices.
But when it's absent, everybody notices.

Warren Buffett, CEO Berkshire-Hathaway Inc.

Little things win big games. Anyone who knows me, and any of my former players, could also tell you that this phrase is the core of my philosophy. In business it is also often the case that little things make a big difference. In both arenas, there must exist a certain attention to detail and focus on the core fundamentals of a task or project to achieve success.

This focus involves teamwork, and with teamwork communication is paramount for success. Organizations invest thousands of training dollars on verbal and electronic communication. Yet even in this wired world, the most important connection is the human connection. The most significant aspect of this connection surprisingly is often unspoken. Researchers at the University of California at Berkeley have proven this on, of all places, the basketball court.

Researchers Michael Kraus, Cassy Huang, and Dacher Keltner spent the entire 2008–2009 season coding three types of nonverbal communication (high fives, hugs, and bumps) on each team in every NBA game. They found that the most successful teams and individual players made more consistent contact with their teammates. To ensure the effect wasn't just seen in teams because they were already winning, the research was focused on the initial months of the season. Longitudinally, the researchers compared the touch totals of perennial power Boston Celtics with that of the Golden State Warriors, a perennial doormat. The Celtics and their leader Kevin Garnett (among the NBA's touchiest players) were quick to touch, in contrast to Golden State, which would go stretches of several minutes without teammates communicating via touch. (It should be noted this research took place right after the Celtics won their most recent championship.)

The results stand to reason when you consider other research on personal touch. Harvard researchers determined the brain development of babies was enhanced by personal touch. University of Miami researcher Tiffany Field determined that students who received a supportive touch on the arm or back by a teacher were almost twice as likely to participate in class as those who didn't. Numerous research studies have shown the power of touch to alleviate anxiety and decrease cortisol levels. Touch has the ability to trigger the release of oxytocin, a hormone that helps create a sense of trust in humans. Trust encourages teammates to take intelligent risks and push the performance envelope. Trust can also help you lead people in directions they might not go on their own. Team cohesion and trust go hand in hand in fostering esprit de corps and members putting forth greater effort.

In discussing this NBA study, Kraus says, *"One of the major touching differences we see is in some of the really good teams when a player has made a negative play, they'll walk over and give him a hand and pull him up. Some of the other teams, you make a negative play, you can be sitting there for several moments and have to get yourself up."*

This data alone should result in a bit of introspection. How often do you "help up" a fallen teammate at work? How do you address the salesperson who has a bad month or the project manager who just made a tactical error? Do your team members only get the proverbial high five after an occasional success? Or is it consistent and frequent regardless of the situation? I am not suggesting the CFO give his accounting team a pat on the fanny because this would pose a serious harassment issue. I am suggesting you stay connected through personal touch. Research indicates that it takes an average of three hours of continuous interaction to reach the same level of rapport you can gain from one single handshake. Clearly even a quick tap on the shoulder in the hallway or a high five across cubicles on a regular basis has value. A feeling of mutual trust can enhance performance in any work environment from the locker room to the board room.

Over the course of your lifetime you have probably been associated with a few highly successful teams and on occasion a couple less-than-successful ones as well. Whether it was a sports team, a military unit, or a project team you were selected for at work, I encourage you to reflect on the interpersonal factors at play on a few of these teams. Forget talent. It isn't an interpersonal factor. Talent is a skill. There is a great likelihood you will attribute trust and respect as key interpersonal factors on your successful teams. I would add that unsuccessful teams are that way due to a lack of trust more often than due to a lack of talent. Talent is common; indeed, talented individuals are a dime a dozen. Trusted teammates on the other hand are not. A go-to-guy in your organization is referred to as such because you trust he will get the job done, not merely because he possesses superior talent.

Knowing the key role trust plays in relationships and on teams, the question then becomes how do you as a leader facilitate a culture of trust within the organization to enhance team chemistry? Chemistry starts with trust, and trust starts at the top. If you want better team chemistry, start with being a trustworthy leader.

Trust is the hardest thing to earn and the easiest thing to lose. Consequently, having a focus on small daily practices of trust and respect helps build a sort of equity with teammates over time. On the court, as the Celtics demonstrate, it may be something as simple as extending a helping hand to pick a teammate up off the floor or a pat on the back when he misses a shot. In the office it may be extending common courtesy to a colleague or sending a thank-you note to a subordinate or a new client. Most people by nature shy away from making a significant commitment to a goal, group, or person due to the fear and risk involved. Trust is the antidote to fear. It breeds confidence and faith both in yourself and in others. When this culture of trust is present, team chemistry can soar to new heights.

Trust is a key element in interpersonal communication. We have used touch since the beginning of time to communicate trust, kindness, and many other human emotions in an expedient way. Research indicates effective communication and good relationships on the job are the number-one factors in happiness in the workplace. Cultivating an office environment rich in happiness can reduce absenteeism, and turnover, and serves to enhance greater productivity and teamwork among staff members.

(National High Five Day is the third Thursday in April.)

Coaching Points

- What steps do you take to build a culture of trust within your team or organization?
- What do the "high fives" in your organization look like?
- When are they distributed and for what?
- When aren't they distributed that they should be?

Chapter 5

Seasons of Business

Sport is human life in microcosm.

Howard Cosell, American sports broadcaster

It is easier to train yourself to be a collegiate or professional athlete than it is to train to become a corporate athlete. If you are struggling with this concept, you are not alone. You are probably wondering how this is possible, considering athletes who have reached this elite level represent the best of the best. They have invested thousands of hours honing and refining their unique skill set, and physically conditioning their bodies to peak performance. After all, they make a living with their athleticism and skills.

It is easier in large part due to the fact that their work is segmented into specific seasons. For example, elite athletes have the benefit of a sizable off-season when they can rest and recover from the demands of the season just completed. The off-season "work schedule" usually is limited and consists of several hours of training or conditioning while the remainder of their time and energy is invested in renewal activities (mental as well as physical). Elite athletes also have a team behind their team to assist them in their professional journey. Exercise physiologists, nutritionists, chefs, masseurs, sport psychologists, and specialized coaches all serve as resources to facilitate the athlete's or team's success.

29

Like a lacrosse game, the fiscal year for the game of business is broken into quarters. Unlike lacrosse's four-month season every spring, the sport of business has no off-season. For virtually everyone, it is a 365-day season. The conclusion of one season is followed immediately by the next. Adding to this recipe for burnout, most business leaders do not enlist the assistance of a team behind their team as athletes do.

Business leaders could better position their organizations for success by taking a page out of the strategic plan coaches follow. NCAA rules mandate a 20-hour weekly maximum for athletic participation by student-athletes. Therefore, coaches have a limited window of time to conduct team activities and training. The 20-hour-a-week NCAA-imposed boundary forces coaches and athletes to work smarter and more efficiently, not longer. Efficiency is the high-octane fuel of peak performance. Business leaders, on the other hand, do not have any limits imposed on their workday or workweek. In the case of some executives I've coached, when we first met, their standard workweek consisted of 60-plus hours and their Blackberry essentially served as a nightlight. I am not suggesting you impose a 20-hour workweek on your organization; however, I do recommend setting reasonable, healthy boundaries.

Many people view the executives I just described as dedicated or committed. I viewed each of these clients as a person who lacked boundaries, discipline, and priorities. By setting tighter boundaries for the work you perform, you are actually committing yourself to enhancing your focus and preventing yourself from burning out. If I told you I coached athletes who spent 12 hours a day in the gym lifting weights, running, performing agility drills, and practicing lacrosse, you wouldn't say they are dedicated; you would say they are overtraining and I was a shortsighted tyrant.

Quite simply, elite athletes perform at such a high level because they understand and value the fact that it takes a great deal of mental acuity and physical fitness to read and react quickly on game day. In examining the rigors of a corporate athlete, the frequency and duration of the demands on the mind and body consistently exceed that of the lacrosse athlete. The sports phrase "fatigue makes cowards of us all" has never been more apropos than with business leaders. When athletes physically fatigue, they become susceptible to mental errors on the field. Elite athletes condition themselves so they not only begin each season in the best shape possible but also so their superior conditioning is the competitive advantage needed to display fourth quarter excellence when their competitors cannot. If you examine late game heroics, you will find a remarkable correlation between the level of conditioning and the magnitude of individual or team performance.

Business professionals are no different, yet a priority is not placed on training the body in a manner that allows the mind to perform at an optimal level. Conditioning in any endeavor also involves the key ingredient of rest and recovery. Additionally, upon conclusion of the season, the athlete has an opportunity to rest, recover, and in some cases rehabilitate from injuries sustained during the season.

Organizations, their departments, and employees all have times of the year when they are busier than others. I prefer to think of this as their "in-season." High performers know exactly where these seasons are on the calendar, and they are prepared for their arrival because they have taken the proper steps in the two prior seasons on their calendar: the off-season and the pre-season.

The off-season is a time where individuals and work teams can, like athletes, devote proper time to rest and recover as well as rehabilitation and professional growth. Without creating a plan to rest (mentally, physically, and emotionally) and then developing strength through professional development, you cannot propel yourself forward with growth. Coaches devote time in the off-season to travel, family vacations, attending and speaking at conferences for professional development, retooling playbooks, strategic planning for the upcoming season, and staff development.

In addition, I cannot emphasize enough the importance of quiet, contemplative thought. Numerous studies show the importance of quiet, uninterrupted thought in stimulating creativity and cultivating clarity of vision and focus. Scheduling such time should be performed during all seasons of your business, but the off-season provides an ideal time to emphasize it and devote additional time to it. The off-season is naturally a time for introspection, examination, re-evaluation, and problem solving in order to create an effective game plan for success in the upcoming season.

Not creating and engaging in an off-season is an opportunity lost and will leave you unprepared for the rigors and challenges of the season. In essence you are not able to maximize your potential, and you will be left at a significant disadvantage compared to competitors who have done so. A great investment in the right off-season activities will yield massive, game-changing results when you are in-season.

Following the off-season is a pre-season period in which you can begin, with better clarity and a renewed focus, to train and prepare in earnest for the challenges and hurdles you will encounter in-season. There is a cumulative effect to seasons. The quality of the efforts and activities from the previous season will have a direct impact on your trajectory as you transition into the next. Perhaps the most critical is transitioning from the off-season to the pre-season. Pre-season affords you an opportunity to put to the test some of your strategic planning and hypotheses developed in the off-season. It also enables you to cross-train employees, practice job rotation, and build bench strength through developing young leaders into new roles as they mature within the organization.

How does an organization or individual effectively identify and plan for the creation of seasons of business? Just like a coach is my answer. Each year I would take critical dates from the season and reverse engineer our strategic plan accordingly. You will want to seek feedback from your team and look for patterns that reveal important sales cycles, productivity cycles, growth cycles, and downtime.

A clear example of this is the retail sales industry. It has a series of in-seasons surrounding holidays on the calendar, with a major in-season taking place between Black Friday and Christmas Eve. In the sport of retailing, those two days alone represent two separate championship games. After these retail championships take place, there is not an immediate off-season. The in-season does wind down a bit as returns and after-Christmas sales conclude. The time after New Year's can be viewed as an off-season of sorts when inventory and floor plans can be reassessed.

Conversely, the financial services industry operates on a very different schedule of seasons. Christina E. White, J.D., CRPC, regional director of training for Ameriprise Financial Services Inc., says, "Holiday time represents an off-season for brokers and financial advisors." She emphasizes that "the major in-season for advisors kicks off in earnest after New Year's when people have made resolutions about their finances and continues through February into the spring months." When late spring transitions into early summer, it is an off-season for their business because clients are often less accessible as vacation schedules come into play. "A preseason mind-set comes into play during late summer as advisors make preparations for their second in-season of the calendar year, which arrives in the fall and continues until the holidays approach." She believes having a good sense of the business development seasons and their ebbs and flows better enables advisors to plan strategically. It facilitates their ability to focus their efforts and energy in the right areas at the right times over the course of the year. Figure 1 gives an example of how I designed the seasons for my team.

Lacrosse Seasons	
September 1 - October 15	Non-Traditional Season (16 practice dates and 1 contest)
October 16 - January 12	Off-Season 2 (Individual Workouts, Strength and Conditioning)
January 13	Official Start Date of Traditional Pre-Season Practices
February 15 - 28	Pre-Season Scrimmages (2)
March 1 - 20	In-Season: Nonconference games (7)
March 21 - April 18	Conference Schedule Portion of Season (6)
April 18 - May 1	Postseason and Conference Tournament (4)
May 28	Conclusion of Season (National Championship Game Date)
May 30 - June 12	Vacation/Family Time
June 13 - August 14	Off-Season 1 (Strategic Planning, Recruiting, Professional Development, Renewal)

Figure 1

I've always had an affinity for using metaphors involving symbolism and visually illustrating concepts for my team. To begin the 2002 academic year, as a team-building and campus beautification project, our soccer coach and I had our teams plant hedges around our stadium. Over the course of the academic year, it was our players' responsibility to feed and water these hedges. This team-building activity served as an excellent embodiment of the concept of seasons, growth cycles, and incremental visible progress over time. The way we had to take care of the hedges differently during each season of the year was a perfect reminder to all of us. If we committed to engaging in the proper activities during the proper seasons, it would serve to fuel our growth and development. Then, come springtime when we were in-season, we would be performing at an optimal level when it mattered most. I encourage you to do the same with your team. Often a leader's repeated message wears on his or her team members and loses its desired effect over time. A subtle yet powerful symbolic illustration of your message will amplify your voice and make it resonate with your people in a manner you alone simply cannot achieve. In our case, the hedges represented us as a team. The soil was our organizational culture; water and sunlight represented our nutritional and training habits. The soil needed to have the right content to promote growth, and without the right habits the shrubs could not effectively develop strong roots. My players quickly understood the analogies to team chemistry and the discipline of our training, and nutritional and social habits.

In the quest for market supremacy, many hard-charging leaders operate under the mistaken premise that results dictate the culture. They think if their team would just work harder and commit to burning the midnight oil, they will win faster or win right away. Then they will have a winning culture. This short-sighted, pressure-packed, unrealistic approach is counterproductive and usually results in a culture that produces undesirable results: burnout, turnover, and poor morale. On any team in any industry, culture drives the bottom line, not the other way around.

What representation of seasons of business will resonate best with your people? If sports seasons will not, perhaps it is using farming as a metaphor for your business. Think of the off-season in your business as the planting season and you are planting seeds of success. Then view your busy season as the harvest. In business and in sport, you reap what you sow. Quite simply, if you sow mediocrity that is what you will also reap. If you feed and water your team daily, figuratively speaking, they can grow to new heights.

Coaching Points

- How do you define your in-season?

- When does your off-season take place? (You may find multiple busy seasons and several short off-seasons as opposed to the schedule above.)

- How do your people engage in rest, recovery, and renewal in-season and during the off-season?

- How do these activities differ?

- What are the expectations for performance during the off-season?

TIME OUT
THE ELITE EIGHT WAYS TO BE AN IMPACT PLAYER

1. Be here now! Be present in the moment, grounded in reality.
2. Little things win big games. Pay attention to the little things that make a big difference.
3. Thrive on accountability and emphasize self-improvement.
4. Focus on fundamentals.
5. To get a clearer picture, see the big picture.
6. See your target, not the obstacles.
7. Be a great teammate. Add value to your relationships.
8. Be early, stay late. Get extra R.E.P.S. (repetition elevates personal skills).

Part III

SECOND QUARTER

Chapter 6

Three Questions

I never learn anything talking.
I only learn things when I ask questions.
Lou Holtz, Hall of Fame college football coach

In 1994, my first year coaching, I was invited to meet former Notre Dame football coach Lou Holtz and listen to him speak about leadership. I was so struck by a three-question test he posed to us regarding leadership that it has served as my compass from that day forward. Holtz shared with us the three questions he believes you need to consider about every person you meet.

1. Can I trust you?
2. Do you care about me?
3. Are you committed to excellence?

As simple as these questions may appear, they cut to the heart of any interpersonal relationship: teammate to teammate, employee to employee, player to coach, and employee to supervisor, to name a few. Think about the mentors in your life, both personal and professional. I would venture to say you could answer yes to all three questions with regard to each of your mentors. Holtz also encouraged us to look at the three-question test from the other person's perspective. Your answers to these questions will begin to probe the roots of any issues that may exist between you and the other person answering those questions about you.

Over the years I have found Holtz's three-question test to be a great tool for me to gain a better understanding of how I relate to and work with people. There were often times I found my answers revealed something I needed to work on.

I believe that the cornerstone of my lacrosse program always positively addressed these three questions. A prime example of this can be found in the way we addressed balancing academics and athletics. Many college coaches and athletic programs focus on the athlete portion of the term "student-athlete" and neglect to place a priority on the student's academic achievement. By consistently articulating and demonstrating our philosophy of developing the whole person, we sent a loud, clear message of precisely how much we cared about the young men in our program. This care and concern helped earn the trust of a variety of constituents, from faculty members and parents of recruits to our alumni and boosters. As these constituents came to learn more about our goals and vision, it quickly became apparent to them just how committed we were to excellence.

Much like the world of collegiate athletics, many organizations in the business world view employees merely as human capital rather than being committed to developing the whole person. When you send the message, directly or indirectly, that the bottom line is the only thing that matters, you do not engender loyalty on the part of your team members. Quite simply, you fail the three-question test at every juncture. Without trust and genuine caring for your team members, there can be no true commitment to excellence. Holtz made the three-question test sequential by design.

From an employee standpoint, seeing how leadership places a value on helping its people maximize their potential both personally and professionally demonstrates in word and deed the organization's care for its people. I once had an opportunity to interview the all-time winningest college basketball coach, the legendary Don Meyer, on this very subject. I was pleased to discover Meyer and I share a similar coaching philosophy, and it is a philosophy that transcends sport. His philosophy or what he calls one of his rules on winning centers on team and individual morale. He said, *"Morale is what motivates the best to get better. There must be a spirit of devotion, enthusiasm, and purpose present on the team. Until you find a higher purpose than winning, you will never win."*

This is a pretty powerful statement on the importance of finding a higher purpose than winning, considering it is coming from the all-time winningest coach in college basketball history (923 career wins). Meyer's belief was that in order to win in sports or business you need to create team chemistry centering on something far greater than a simple outcome. In order to maintain that chemistry, everyone must buy in to it and maintain that buy-in on a daily basis. I believe the best way to achieve this is through developing a team covenant.

I have never been a big believer in corporate mission statements, slogans, and core values that you often see prominently displayed at the main entrance or inside the lobby of office buildings. These mission statements, values, and slogans are, at best, for the customer to see. At worst, they are misguided and merely window dressing. Take for example Enron's mission statement: *"Respect, Integrity, Communication, and Excellence."* Based on the behaviors of Enron's employees at multiple levels within the organization, these four words were merely terms plastered on the entrance to the lobby and the homepage of its website. They were not a value system, nor did this statement provide the people within the organization with any kind of description of what those four words each look like in action.

A core covenant differs from a mission statement or a set of core values because a covenant speaks to not only the essence of who you are as an organization but also to what the living, breathing embodiment of that looks like in action each day. At the beginning of each year, I would ask my players in individual meetings what they felt were the cornerstones or, as Coach Meyer would call it, the higher purpose of our program. I would compile the answers. This provided me with a great measuring stick of what the players valued and how each of their values aligned with one another. In other words, how close were they to being on the same page at the beginning of the year? As a team, we would develop a document that would serve as the cornerstones of our program for that year. The document would not merely list the cornerstones of our program but also describe how they each looked in action.

For example, in 2002 one of the cornerstones of our program was dedication. Before the year began, we felt we had the potential to have a very special season, but the only way to turn potential to performance would be through dedication not just by "being dedicated" but also by each person dedicating his efforts to a higher purpose. So each member of the team dedicated his season to someone special who had made an impact on his life. I dedicated the 2002 season to my father who had lost his battle with cancer two weeks before the season began. In order to be a living, breathing embodiment of dedication we needed to define exactly how dedication looked in the daily lives of our players. Figure 2 gives an example of dedication in action.

Dedication

What does a dedicated student-athlete do in the classroom?

- Arrive early, sit in the front of the classroom, ask questions
- Be at or near perfect attendance
- Be organized and prepared for each class
- Maintain excellent grades
- Get extra tutoring when needed

What does a dedicated student-athlete do on the field?

- Arrive early, stay late, ask questions
- Be mentally and physically prepared at every practice and game
- Maintain excellent physical fitness
- Trust and support teammates and coaches
- Get extra reps in on your own or with a coach

What does a dedicated student-athlete do in the community?

- "B.A.G."= Be A Gentleman
- Help the less fortunate
- Be a role model for younger students
- Protect the team

Figure 2

Dedication was not only a cornerstone of our program, but it also served as our trigger word to reflect on when adversity hit, when in a slump, or when we had to find the reserves in the tank to push through late in a game. I think it worked. We advanced to the NCAA Final Four, had our first winning season, and six of our ten wins were one-goal games. And we finished the season ranked third in the country.

You will find that empowering your people to develop a team covenant not only clarifies what is truly important and how to go about achieving it but also provides them ownership of the cornerstones of the organization. How do your people embody the cornerstones of your organization in the office, in the business community, and in serving the greater good of your community?

A covenant will also bring about greater clarity to the three-question test. You are demonstrating care by taking your team members through the exercise of creating the covenant. In doing so you are exercising a great deal of trust through the process of empowering them to determine these cornerstones. Lastly, holding one another accountable for being a living, breathing embodiment of the team covenant sends a clear signal of your commitment to excellence.

Coaching Points

- Look at the people in your department or on your team. Apply Holtz's three-question test. How do they measure up?

- Look at the leader you see in the mirror. How do you measure up?

- Can you clearly and concisely articulate the cornerstones of your organization?

- What do they look like in action?

- How do you think your team would answer the last two questions?

Chapter 7

Win the Whistles

The team that makes the most mistakes will probably win.
The doer makes mistakes and I want doers on my team –
players who make things happen.
John Wooden, Coaching icon and Basketball Hall of Famer

"Commission not omission!" Those words have been permanently lodged in my brain by my first lacrosse coach, John Distler. He was talking about errors, and at age 15, I thought it seemed odd that he encouraged them. Not only did he encourage them, he encouraged them in quantity. It wasn't until years later that I fully understood why.

If you are going to make a mistake, it is better for you to commit a physical error where you are going full speed than make a mental error where you omitted something in the process. There is sound logic in this philosophy because when you commit an error, at least you are exactly that— committed to what you are doing. Contrast that with the lack of commitment that marks an error of omission. We want engaged employees, and we want committed friends and spouses. We want engagement from our employees and commitment in our relationships. Our regrets in life are a lot like errors, we regret most that which we neglected to attempt rather than things we did do. Business and life mirror sport once again.

47

My coaching mentors' wisdom rubbed off on me in several ways. Attention to detail and Coach Distler's "Wooden-esque" philosophy on mistakes in particular. While I am a stickler for details, there were a few things on the field I was okay with when they went wrong. Special teams and special situations in sports like lacrosse are often the difference makers in close games. None are more important in many sports than face-offs. Winning face-offs equals possessions, and possessions result in goals. Therefore we focused a lot of our efforts in practice on facing off. Every day our face-off specialists would head out to practice ten minutes early to practice an array of face-off drills. We had them responding to whistles and also practicing with no whistle, just reacting to the opposing player's movement in order to improve their reaction time, technique, and countermoves.

When facing off, the goal is to react to the official's whistle before the opponent in order to get a competitive advantage in gaining possession of the ball. I call it winning the whistle. The face-off is equal parts art, science, and instinct. Consequently I always made a conscious effort to teach technique, and then get out of the way and not over coach. From time to time in games, our players would false start on the face-off. A false start occurs when you react before the whistle has blown. This results in the ball being awarded to the other team.

Although false starts are errors, they are errors of commission not omission. As a coach, I can live with that. While I do not want my players consistently false starting, I do want them anticipating the whistles, and a false start indicates just that. It is feedback that tells me the athlete is at his edge. He's ensuring he does not waste a single fraction of a second that could be the difference between winning control of the ball and losing it. This is where the instinctual aspects of the face-off kick in. It is the right instinct. While his timing may be slightly off, it is slightly off in the right direction.

As a leader you strive to reduce and eliminate errors and failures in your team's operation. The reality is failure happens from time to time. It is not the failure that is important as much as it is the response to the failure. Organizations and leaders have a natural tendency to assign blame for mistakes and failure. By assigning blame or attempting to correct or teach them what went wrong you are sending a message to the individual responsible that failure is not acceptable. A by-product of this message is finger pointing. Knowing blame will be assigned or other punitive measures will be imposed causes employees to begin the blame game. They try to paint an alternative reality in which the mistake wasn't their fault simply to save face or preserve their own ego.

I assure you this won't result in more whistles won. On the contrary, it will make your people more cautious. Opportunities will be missed due to errors of omission because teammates won't attempt certain undertakings for fear of failure. While success teaches a lot, failure teaches even more.

Oftentimes I've had the urge to say something to a player when he came off the field right after making a mistake and he beat me to it. The fact of the matter is that most of the time, players know they made a mistake and don't need to hear it from me. They feel even worse about it than I do because they lived the experience and know how it impacts others on the team. By allowing them the space to work through the problem and showing them unconditional support, I've created an environment where they have space to problem solve and work it out on their own. If you recruited the people to do a job and you feel you did a good job evaluating their talent, you owe it to them to provide them with that support.

That being said, the leader owes it to himself and the organization to take a long hard look at how these errors are occurring and examine the response. Are they errors of commission or omission? How did you address the errors or failures after they happened? Did you treat them like feedback and use them as teachable moments or were they simply used to make an example of someone in a punitive way?

Particularly in the early years of my coaching career, there were a number of conversations I wish I could have back and do over. The potentially teachable moments in the heat of battle instead were punitive for the team member. I benched or berated players for taking a costly penalty or committing an error in timing. The decision to handle the situation in that manner came from my reacting instead of responding. I reacted with my heart instead of my head. Emotionally I was frustrated with the player, so I let him have it. In my head, I knew deep down that an experienced, elite athlete wouldn't intentionally do something so foolish.

One particular moment stands out above all others, a closely contested playoff game vs.archrival Limestone College in 2002. My face-off specialist Scott Gordon, after losing a critical face-off late in the game, got a penalty for delivering a hit from behind. His foul caused us to be short-handed for one minute at a time when we were down by three goals and needed to regain possession of the ball. I was annoyed because, in the heat of battle, I thought he lashed out at the player in frustration. I thought he was being selfish. We had the game within reach and just needed a couple of quality scoring opportunities to tie the game. When Scott came off the field, I let him have it and laced into him for being selfish and foolish. I asked him what the hell he was thinking! To his credit, Scott calmly looked me in the eyes and said, "Coach, it's me Scott, your senior captain. I wasn't being selfish. It was a hustle foul. Nobody on our defense picked him up so I chased him down and made sure he didn't score. You and I both know we have one of the best penalty killing units in the country, so I took the penalty. That's what I was thinking." I realized then that my reaction was emotional. Had I opted to respond on an intellectual level,

I would have told him, "Shake it off, I know why you did what you did. That was a good penalty to take."

The beauty of the story was at the tail end of his response while serving the penalty. "Watch coach. Our man down unit is gonna kill this penalty and get the ball back. Put me back in and I will score." Sure enough, 45 seconds into the foul, our penalty killing unit lives up to its reputation, makes a stop, and regains possession of the ball. The penalty ends, and I substitute Scott's midfield line back in the game. Our attack unit gets him the ball right away for an isolation play, and he scores. The lesson for the leader, there is a lot to be said for listening to your best people and letting them find their edge. There's also a lot to be said for the instincts of teammates knowing whom they can count on in crunch time and getting him the ball.

The reality of it is that if you haven't made a few mistakes, you haven't really coached. The same is true in business with leadership. If you haven't made a few mistakes, you haven't really led. The teacher needs to learn from the teachable moment that escaped him and make sure that in the future it is used to enhance, not impair, performance.

Coaching Points
- What does winning the whistle look like in your industry?
- How do you know when an employee is operating at his edge?
- How can you provide employees with the space to work through the problem yet also share feedback in the form of a teachable moment?
- Can your team identify its go-to guys? Can you?

Chapter 8

Opening Rituals

Every day is a new opportunity.
You can build on yesterday's success or put its failures
behind and start over again.
Bob Feller, Hall of Fame major league baseball pitcher

In business as in a lacrosse game, you can't afford to have poor starts. They put you in a negative frame of mind and force you to play from behind early on the scoreboard and on the clock. You are unnecessarily handicapping yourself from the onset. This ground is difficult to make up later. Many a game, sale, interview, and presentation have been lost due to a poor start.

Why do individuals and teams have slow starts or poor starts? I attribute it primarily to nerves and fear. Fear prevents you from taking action and impairs performance very quickly. In both my coaching and consulting careers I have yet to find a saboteur of success quite as effective as fear. Even with a well-laid-out plan, fear can wreak havoc on your start. I am not necessarily referencing fear of failure. In some cases it may be a fear of success. Fear redirects your focus from the positive to the negative. Specifically, it diverts you away from being present in the moment and working your process.

The best way to counteract this negative emotion and remove fear is to create and employ the power of opening rituals and routines. In effect, rituals and routines serve to prime the pump for performance. On the field, successful coaches and teams utilize opening rituals to make sure they get off to a strong start. It sets the tone for all performance moving forward in the game. The million-dollar question is how do you ensure your team gets off to a strong start? I have found enormous value in rituals for creating positive momentum.

Opening rituals can take many forms. The primary objective of each is to bring about clarity and focus and to facilitate the individual operating at peak performance. An effective opening ritual will provide the athlete or businessperson with positive energy, positive visual images and outcomes, as well as feelings of confidence, strength, and control. It can also be a focusing technique to minimize nervous energy or "nerves." Clear focus produces clear action.

On the lacrosse field, our opening ritual on the first possession of a game was always a set play we called "opener." This play changed each week as it was designed to simultaneously exploit the weakness of that particular opponent's defense while also playing to our offensive strengths. The impact of "striking early" and beginning a game with a 1-0 lead cannot be underestimated. The only thing better than striking early is striking early and often. Over the years, my teams became known for getting off to quick starts. This was often a topic of conversation by my opponents and became part of the scouting report on my teams. The beauty of getting off to a strong start is that by manufacturing small success or momentum you are better able to attract additional success. In essence momentum begets momentum. Think of a time you made a good sale; the next sale came a lot quicker and easier, didn't it?

While practicing our opener each week, I would also incorporate visualization into my players' practice routines.

Visualization stimulates the power of the subconscious mind and actually serves to help program the reticular activating system, or R.A.S. The reticular activating system is, in layman's terms, like a processing unit for data being input in our "hard drives" (brains). Scientists believe the R.A.S. processes pictures more efficiently than words. Therefore, picturing successful execution of a task over and over again will not only strengthen your belief but also facilitate the actual execution of that task.

My use of opening rituals was not limited to game day; I incorporated them into each aspect of performance to set the stage for proper focus and being present in the moment. Opening rituals serve as a conscious transition from one activity to another. This transition is essential in maintaining focus. Recent research debunks the myth about the greatness of multitasking. In reality, we are far more productive individually and as teams when we are able to apply a singleness of purpose to our activity. When you are able to focus, you are better able to respect the process, thus facilitating a more successful result.

Think of the ways you can utilize opening rituals as a focusing tool or to manufacture positive momentum with your department or in your personal work environment. The opening ritual formula is one I use with my clients as a tool to capture their focus at the onset of our meeting. It is essentially a transitional check-in consisting of five steps.

1. How are you doing?

2. This is the start of our work together; everything outside of our work is exactly that, outside. This is our time together. Let us maximize it.

3. Here is what I see as our purpose. Please share yours.

4. Here is what we will be working on. (Based on purpose shared in number three.)

5. Clarification of our major points of emphasis.

This is a helpful process because it provides the clients with whom I work a conscious transition into our work environment. It is my job to utilize every tool available to capture and maintain their focus and attention. Over the years, I have found this to be the most effective method. For purposes of comparison I include a team opening ritual formula I have utilized. I use the mantra "Win The Day" to help focus on the task immediately at hand.

1. Check-in. How are we doing on a scale of 0-5?
2. Opening comments: theme, focus of practice or meeting.
3. Statement of purpose and Win The Day goal (why we are here).
4. Highlight major points of emphasis.
5. Quick team feedback and comments.

As you can see, it is remarkably similar to the opening ritual I use to create a conscious transition when meeting with individual clients. An opening ritual with a group or team goes beyond just creating an awareness of being present in the moment to creating a connection, aligning the group, and fostering a sense of fellowship. It provides individuals with a process by which to move beyond their own situations and unite. This transition is absolutely mission-critical because before your team members arrive at the office, they may have already had a morning filled with crisis, problem solving, interpersonal conflict, personal/family issues, or perhaps a grueling commute. Understandably, their minds may be elsewhere.

Opening rituals are equally effective in enhancing individual workplace performance. In an interview with athletic administrator and thought leader Dan Cardone, I learned of an outstanding workplace opening ritual that he practices daily. He doesn't call it an opening ritual, rather it is simply how he starts each day. As an administrator at North Hills High School in Pennsylvania, he feels an obligation to help maintain high morale amongst his staff. Cardone says, "Maintaining high morale is a key to peak performance." I couldn't agree more. He engages in a daily exercise he calls five before nine, where his goal is to share sincere thanks and appreciation of a job well done with five people before 9 a.m. Cardone will not set foot in his office until he has done so each morning. One example he shared was thanking the groundskeepers who maintain the turf in the stadium, line the fields, and mow the grass on campus. I love this example because maintenance is one of the most important yet simultaneously underappreciated jobs in any organization. The maintenance staff members are the directors of first impressions at any facility, and as we know in business, first impressions can make or break any deal. Sharing sincere appreciation demonstrates to them not only that their hard work did not go unnoticed but also that their role on the team is important and valued. (If you do not know your maintenance staff on a first name basis, I highly recommend you get to know them immediately.)

As I reflected on Cardone's strategy, I became so fond of it that I began incorporating it into my daily opening ritual. As a solo practitioner, on most days I cannot make my rounds and thank or congratulate five people face to face. Instead I have incorporated a 5 by 9 gratitude ritual where I express appreciation or congratulations to five people by 9 a.m. in the form of handwritten thank-you notes, letters, and personal phone calls.

My own workplace "opener" is a series of the following daily opening rituals.

1. Clear desk, clear mind.

2. Do a concentration or meditation exercise.

3. Read or listen to something positive and inspirational.

4. Examine the task list I assembled at the close of the previous day.

5. Visualize successful execution of tasks.

6. Do the 5 by 9 gratitude exercise.

While each element is valuable in setting the stage for strong performance, I have found Cardone's 5 by 9 exercise most valuable. Investing a few minutes at the start of each day in writing notes of congratulations or appreciation to clients and colleagues consciously brings me into a positive frame of mind. This shift to a positive mind-set is consistent regardless of what may have happened prior to arriving at my office. The human mind is not capable of simultaneously holding a negative thought and a positive one. Therefore, by intentionally opening my workday on a positive note, I fill my mind with gratitude, appreciation, successful images, and positive outcomes. It also provides me with a sense of control.

This is the difference between a reaction and the right action. Opening rituals are a much more proactive action than, for example, starting your workday by reading and reacting to emails, which depending on the content can quickly send your mind-set and mood into a tailspin. Beyond expressing appreciation, a gratitude ritual can also be a valuable new business development tool. Sending a handwritten thank-you to a prospect or client you just met with can make a powerful statement about you and your values. Consider the impression you are making on the client. Thoughtful, appreciative, attentive to detail, disciplined follow-up skills, and willing to go the extra mile are all qualities that come to mind.

Success does not happen by itself, and when it does happen, it certainly isn't ever by accident. Business leaders today have become so results-oriented and bottom-line driven that they overlook the fundamentals of what makes for successful performance. Whether you are a college athlete or a corporate athlete, you can employ the power of ritual to facilitate success.

Engaging in ritual is not wasting or spending valuable time, rather it is an investment in the power of attention and intention. When you make an investment, it yields dividends. The typical businessperson's day is overscheduled. When factoring in 24-7 technology and cell phone access, it becomes that much more difficult to be present in the moment. This is all the more reason to harness the performance power of ritual and engage in the art of monotasking. Keep in mind that when it comes to opening rituals, simple is better, and to achieve consistent positive results, it should be employed consistently every day.

Coaching Points

- How fast do you or your team start?

- Do you have a process for beginning the workday or beginning a team meeting/activity?

- What does "striking early" look like in your business? How can you consistently do so?

- What is the most effective way you can bring yourself into a performance mind-set to begin each day?

Chapter 9

Success Rituals

What to do with a mistake: recognize it, admit it,
learn from it, and then forget it.

Dean Smith, Hall of Fame college basketball coach

In sport and in business, mistakes are part of the game.
All-Americans make them. Millionaires make them, too. What
separates the top performers from the rest of the competition
is the champion's mind-set. That is, they move past mistakes
immediately, learn from them, and do not fear making them.

There is a difference between playing to win and playing
not to lose. When athletes are playing to win, they do not fear
making mistakes and give 100 percent effort. When athletes are
playing not to lose, they get conservative and tight, and try to
minimize risk for fear of failure. This strategy is self-defeating.
What usually occurs is precisely what they're trying to avoid, a
mistake.

Fear makes mistakes and failure more probable. The error
then is dwelled on and impairs future performances. Does this
sound familiar to you in your job? For example, you may have
worried about how you would handle a big sales presentation
or important client meeting. As a result, when the moment
arrives, you start to over think what to say and how to say it
instead of just communicating. Sure enough, the words come

out all wrong. Then the mind dwells on what was said, and you begin to worry about the other person's judgment of what just took place instead of focusing on what you should be doing next. Or perhaps your fear of failure stems from being browbeaten by an overbearing manager who criticizes every little mistake and shortcoming you and members of your team make. In either scenario, factors like loss of focus, fear, miscommunication, and just plain trying too hard may have contributed to the fear of failure.

How many times have you seen an athlete make a mistake and the coach reacts with total disgust or visible frustration? The player hears and sees the coach's reaction and immediately begins playing tight and tentatively, fearing a similar response from the coach in the event of another error. This is also a common workplace occurrence. The employee makes a mistake, and the manager reacts with disappointment and frustration. The natural consequence of this is the employee performing under fear of future errors and second-guessing herself at critical times, or paralysis by analysis. In other words, what gets thought about gets brought about.

The reality is that mistakes and failure are a natural part of the learning curve. There is an unrealistic and overused "motivational" expression in sport and business that I believe is incomplete. The expression is *Failure is not an option.* This is perhaps the most uninformed and unrealistic point of view any leader can endorse. I prefer the statement *Failure is not an option, it is required.* Failure is a necessary part of the process of achieving success, and to set the expectation within your organization that it is not an option is self-defeating. You are in essence teaching your team to fear failure, which brings about paralysis by analysis. It is the business equivalent of playing not to lose instead of playing to win.

Early in my coaching career I learned a sports psychology strategy called "a mistake ritual." It's a strategy created by college football coaching legend Frosty Westering. Jim Thompson,

CEO of the Positive Coaches Alliance, has gone on to adopt Westering's strategy for letting go of mistakes in order to focus on success as part of its coaches certification program. I have used the strategy as a coach since 1994 and continue to use it now my consulting practice. I believe the term "mistake" has a negative connotation, so I prefer to think of this as a success ritual.

Success rituals are one of the most effective and valuable performance enhancement strategies you can employ. They are so effective because they are multisensory in nature. They are multisensory in that they are not only a physical activity you perform but also visual and possibly auditory as well. Great coaches and educators know that the more senses involved in an activity, the more its effectiveness increases.

A success ritual is a way to remove mistakes from your mind and focus on success. Coach Westering coined the expression "flush it," which you would often hear him telling his players from the sidelines. This was in reference to his mistake ritual of having players visualize flushing the mistake or negative event they just experienced down the toilet in order to clear their mind of the negative image and emotions that were created. A major component of the ritual is to incorporate a physical gesture or motion into it. In this case it would be the individual making the motion of flushing a toilet with his hand. If you were to visit Westering's office at Pacific Lutheran University, you would find a realistic looking, miniature toy toilet that when you press the handle makes a flushing sound. (The same thing can also be found on the bookshelf in my office.)

Westering popularized this ritual that many sports psychologists and coaches use today. Other popular mistake rituals you may see on television include the famous chopping wood gesture Rutgers University football coach Greg Schiano had his players use, a no-sweat gesture where athletes wipe the sweat off their forehead, and a brush-it-off gesture like brushing dust off their arm.

I love the metaphor of flushing a mistake because it is quick, easy to use in any setting, and speaks to the type of content we want to rid our minds of. Peak performers in any industry live in the moment, and success rituals are a major part of what helps them focus on that moment. It is an engagement strategy that helps them rebound and focus their mind in the present moment. A success ritual can also serve as a great coaching tool in any setting because it is a signal a leader or teammates can flash someone at a critical time to remind them to refocus on the present.

How do you know when your team has bought into the concept of a success ritual? You know when you see them using it, more specifically using it to coach each other and you! The best example of team buy-in I have seen is when my team lost in the conference championship and my players noticed how dejected and visibly disappointed I was on the bus ride home. They approached me as a group in the locker room after the game, brought the game film over to the toilet, and literally told me to flush it. Suffice it to say, the teacher was proud to be the student that day. We did flush it, refocused, and went on to compete in regionals, advancing to the semifinals, and playing our best game ever when we lost to the eventual champions.

We have all heard the expression "put your game face on." Employing an effective success ritual will help you maintain your game face in business because beyond staying present in the moment, it is a tool to help maintain emotional control.

Reflect on what usually happens after you make a mistake, whether it is slicing your tee shot deep into the woods on the golf course or making a mistake while delivering your state of the company address to the board of directors. What do you look like after making a mistake? Read through the checklist in Figure 3, and choose your corresponding answers.

Mistake Responses

Posture (slumped over or upright)

Hands (in pockets, thrown up in the air, or at your side)

Head (hanging low or held high with chin up)

Facial Expressions (frown, lips pursed, or smile)

Voice (your tone changes or remains consistent)

Self-Talk (the little voice in your head makes negative remarks or reaffirming ones)

Eyes (looking down, rolling them, or looking up and maintaining contact with the other person)

Breathing (your pattern and rate of breathing increases or remains consistent)

Figure 3

If you answered with any of the first options, you need to develop a success ritual.

Consider for a moment how one of the best performers in your position responds to mistakes and adversity. What does the ideal performance look like after a mistake? How does that person respond? The best performers will consistently respond with confidence, determination, and a sense of what I call "instant amnesia." My friend and colleague Dr. Adam Naylor, sports psychologist at Boston University, has perhaps the best definition of what great players do. He says, "Great players have long-term memories for success and short-term memories for failure." I believe you can insert financial advisors, sales professionals, CEOs, and any other occupation in place of the word "players" and his wisdom will remain true.

How we act after a negative outcome such as a mistake or event determines our ability to flush it. If you go through the motions of the success ritual yet your body language is not congruent with what you do, your ability to refocus will be limited. In my coaching of success rituals, I incorporate a five-second rule. A total of five seconds is all the attention I will allow myself to give the event. In that five seconds I will acknowledge the mistake/event, flush it, and then focus on standing up tall, looking up, taking action, and regulating my breathing. The acronym I use as a reminder is SLAB, which stands for Stand up-Look up-Act-Breathe. This process creates congruence between the success ritual and the appropriate response.

I should add a disclaimer to the success ritual. There is one part of the mistake or negative event that you do want to remember, the part that teaches you. You don't merely want to forget these events, you want to learn from them as well. Just understand that during the heat of battle is not the ideal time to learn from it. Shortly thereafter, while the event is still top of mind and fresh, you can conduct your own performance review, document the lessons learned, and apply them moving forward. Failure is not to be looked at as dead end, rather it is a detour on the road to success.

Coaching Points

- What does playing to win look like in your business?

- It is not an event that defines you, rather how you respond to the event that defines you. How do you currently respond to mistakes and negative events?

- Create your own success ritual using a multisensory approach. Flushing it is a metaphor that speaks to me. What speaks best to you?

- How can you change your response to your team members' mistakes and failures to better coach them on reframing the event?

Chapter 10

Closing Rituals

Bob's a special kind of friend. The kind that drives you crazy!

Dr. Leo Marvin, Psychiatrist

While opening rituals are useful for priming performance and preparing you mentally for the task ahead, closing rituals serve the opposite purpose. They serve to bring closure in a meaningful and positive way to performance.

A closing ritual is akin to flipping a switch to turn our brain off of work and be present in the moment when we transition to other things. Its use does not have to be restricted to sports, work life, or the end of the day. It can be used as a conscious transition from one activity to another in any facet of our lives. The ability to call time out, reflect, and then consciously direct our focus to the next activity facilitates greater ability to be present in the moment. Closing rituals serve the purpose of an intentional daily transition between your professional and personal life.

Many times when we leave work at the end of the day, we take work home with us. Not actual physical work, rather the emotional baggage of work. Consequently, when we are physically at home, our minds still have not left the office. As important as employee engagement is in the workplace, employee disengagement outside of the office is equally important. If you list what needs to be done for tomorrow and the remainder of the week, the very act of placing items on paper removes them from your conscious thought process. This process helps keep you from thinking about work-related tasks after you leave work. Beyond bringing closure to a task, closing rituals should help you focus on the positive and celebrate success you have experienced.

Setbacks in sports and in business are frequent, particularly in pursuit of ambitious, challenging goals. Without a process to document the small wins along the way, there is a natural tendency for people to become discouraged. Dr. David Burns in his book *Feeling Good* talks about the importance of keeping track of and celebrating the minor achievements in our lives. In short, seeking and celebrating small successes are good for our emotional health.

One of the principles of cognitive behavioral therapy involves breaking down goals or projects into bite-sized pieces that can be accomplished one step at a time. The movie What About Bob, starring Bill Murray as therapy patient Bob Wiley, provides us with a great reminder of this. Bob's psychiatrist, Dr. Leo Marvin, treats him for multiphobic personality disorder by teaching him to use baby steps or to set small, reasonable goals for himself one day at a time. Dr. Marvin's memorable quote about his client is that "Bob is a special kind of friend; the kind that drives you crazy!"

Our goals tend to become the Bobs in our professional lives, and we all need a Dr. Marvin of sorts. Once we master the transition from crawling to walking as toddlers, we tend to forget how to take baby steps as we grow up. The media and our instant gratification society tend to sensationalize experts and famous people as overnight successes. In reality these overnight successes are 20 years in the making, and they got there by taking a series of not hundreds but thousands upon thousands of baby steps.

Sometimes looking at the big picture goal and all the steps involved can be daunting. Much like the benefits of frequent, consistent exercise have a cumulative effect on us over time, so does celebrating our small successes on daily basis. There is a famous quote that comes to mind. It has been attributed to everyone from Lao Tzu to Napoleon Hill, but regardless of the originator, it rings true: "Inch by inch life is a cinch, yard by yard it's hard." I believe the inch-by-inch process refers to our small victories.

In 2010 Teresa Amabile and Steven Kramer published a study in the Harvard Business Review on what really motivates workers. They surveyed managers asking them what they think motivates their people the most. The managers reported that they believed recognition to be the number-one factor motivating workers. This survey came on the heels of Amabile and Kramer's longitudinal research studying knowledge workers, surveying them on what the top motivator of their performance was. Interestingly, recognition was ranked last by the workers themselves. The top-ranking factor that motivated them was progress in their jobs. They compared the workers' ratings of their emotions and motivation to the amount of progress made each workday. Through this research they were able to determine that making progress at work was associated with positive emotions and high motivation more than any other workplace activity.

This research confirms my belief that to a large extent we control our own job satisfaction and motivation through goal setting. When we set realistic, attainable goals and create an intentional process to seek and celebrate incremental progress or success, we stand to greatly enhance our own motivation on the job. Progress drives motivation, which in turn drives greater future progress. How are you taking baby steps? Do you have a process of recording and celebrating them?

It is important to invest time at the end of the day to reflect on the process of your day. By building an appointment with yourself into your daily schedule, at day's end you are better able to bring clarity to your progress through introspection. This time can be a critical examination of what worked well and what didn't, formulation of new ideas, and an opportunity to plan for tomorrow. Success leaves clues. If we don't stop to reflect on what went well today and what we need to do better tomorrow, we are overlooking valuable keys to improved performance.

Journaling provides us with a release and brings about a sense of closure. It is therapeutic to recount what was effective and ineffective about the day. Additionally, journaling enables us to better see and remember the small victories. We have a tendency to forget small successes we accomplish on the journey to achieve bigger goals. Doing so can derail us from our bigger goals and objectives. The reality is that remembering these small successes not only closes the day on a positive note but also motivates us to look forward to tomorrow and stay the course.

I had a formula for daily closing rituals with my team. We would utilize closing rituals in practice to bring closure to our day's work on the lacrosse field. It was a bridge for my players from their work as athletes back to their primary purpose as students.

We would huddle at the end of practice and as a team discuss:

- What went successfully and why?
- What areas need additional focus by the team?
- What do our goals for tomorrow need to be?
- Great successes. For example, practice player of the day, exceptional examples of teamwork and leadership, outstanding offensive and defensive efforts, and intangibles.
- Cross the line (explained below)

I refer to the gate at the entrance to the stadium as the line of concentration. When players cross over the line where the concrete ends and the turf begins to enter practice, it signifies a time and place where they can go to as a haven from the problems of the day, no distractions or emotional baggage from earlier in the day is to get carried with them across the line. At the end of practice, I'd ask our players that as they cross back over the line of concentration let practice go out of mind, get away from the game, and focus on the next important task of the day or evening. I now encourage my clients to find their own line of concentration to cross and make that an intentional daily transition point back to their personal life. Many report that doorways, elevators, and stairways leaving their offices make for great lines of concentration, both on their way in and on their way out of work.

Create a symbolic ritual that brings closure to the day and celebrates success. It can be journaling, meditation, exercising, or turning on relaxing music to channel your concentration away from work. I am partial to participating in an activity that encourages you to be present in the moment and celebrate daily success as opposed to focusing on what went wrong or what tasks are piled up for tomorrow.

Quite simply, I have found that the best leaders seek and celebrate small daily success, both for themselves and for their people. I formulated a success strategy for leaders to do this with their teams. It is based on powerful yet simple parenting lessons involving two highly successful people: Sara Blakely and Bart Conner.

Sara Blakely is the CEO and founder of Spanx, one of the world's leading women's hosiery companies. When Blakely was a child, over dinnertime conversation her father would ask her and her siblings what they failed at that day. When they shared their failure with him, he would congratulate them. If any of them didn't have a good tale of failure, her father was disappointed. There is real genius in the reverse psychology her dad used. He taught them during their formative years that one should not fear failure. Failure is necessary because it is feedback and is an expected part of the journey of life.

He showed her at an early age how failure is the process you have to go through to find success. Consequently for Blakely, failure became something she sought out rather than feared. The lesson for every leader is that failure is not an outcome for your people, it is part of the process on the path to success.

The second story was shared with me by one of my mentors, author Jon Gordon. It is about Bart Conner, arguably the most accomplished Olympic gymnasts in U.S. history. Connors' parents took an alternate approach to Blakely's. When he was a child, his parents would ask him every night when they put him to bed what his success of the day was. His father's rationale behind this was if Bart focused on his success as a final thought at bedtime, he would go to bed a success every single night, which automatically meant that he would wake up thinking he was a success each morning. When Conner tore his bicep muscle nine months before the 1984 Olympic Games and team doctors told him he would never make it back in time to compete, he didn't listen to them. He knew in his heart he was going to make it back because his parents helped him see that he was a success every day of his life. Not only did he make it back, he won two Olympic gold medals.

I have adapted the Blakely and Conner success strategies in my consulting and executive coaching. While these conversations may seem little things, little things win big games in sports and in business. When I was coaching, I taught my athletes that practice is like a daily deposit in the bank. When game day arrives, there are then ample funds to draw from for success. Today my clients receive the same coaching, because daily deposits of success accrue interest and pay dividends over time. In my work with clients, I have noticed that organizations often get so caught up in the day-to-day routine of work, they don't take the time to seek and celebrate small successes.

I provide my clients and their teams with a success journal I have published entitled *3 by 5*. I have them journal (deposit) three successes daily prior to 5 p.m. as well as one thing to improve upon to win the following day. In business, as in an athletic contest, there is positive momentum and negative momentum. Are you moving forward toward your goal or being sidetracked away from it? By journaling three successes by 5 o'clock, you are guaranteeing laser-sharp focus on winning the day, which propels you toward your goals. The beauty of journaling your success is that when you take action and stay focused on what truly matters, you create positive momentum. And as you know, momentum creates momentum. Additionally, in the event you hit an obstacle or negative momentum, you can refer back to your many deposits in the journal as a focusing tool to return to a positive mind-set.

This can be a private journal, or as some of my clients do, teams and departments can huddle at the end of the day and share success stories. There was a study conducted by the *Journal of Sports Sciences* that examined how soccer teams' morale and championing affected their ability to win. Research indicated that the teams that celebrated goals with the most exuberance won more. Author Dr. Gert-Jan Pepping concluded, *"The more convincingly someone celebrates their success with their teammates, the greater the chances that team will win."* Clearly sharing successes with colleagues can help create team momentum in any industry, and nothing succeeds like success.

Coaching Points

- Do you finish the day strong?
- How can you make a more effective conclusion to the day's work to disengage and also show yourself you "Won The Day"?
- Win The Day is my mantra. What will be yours?
- How are you seeking and celebrating small successes?

TIME OUT
THE SWEET 16 PERFORMANCE RITUALS

1. Wake up at the same time every morning (early) and make your bed.

2. Exercise and eat breakfast every morning.

3. Practice yoga or tai chi or do some stretching.

4. Maintain an attitude of gratitude. Create a ritual where you give thanks to people who have helped you along the way. (Thank-you cards, emails, phone calls, take the person to lunch.)

5. Reflect. Dedicate time at the beginning of your day for contemplative thought. Do this before turning on electronic devices or answering phones and emails.

6. Visualize the success you want to have that day.

7. Call timeout. Take a brief "brain break" every 20 minutes to refresh and refocus.

8. Schedule recovery time. Take a break every 90 minutes during the workday in order to re-energize, re-center, or make a conscious transition between tasks.

9. Spend time outdoors at lunchtime. (Eat outside, go for a walk, meditate, work out).

10. Hydrate. Drink water consistently throughout the day.

11. Eat five or six small balanced meals daily.

12. Reframe any failures of the day as feedback, and document a lesson learned that will enhance future performance.

13. W.T.D. (Win The Day): Plan your tomorrow before you leave the office today. Identify the one area of focus needed to win the day tomorrow.

14. Keep a journal and write in it daily.

15. Go to bed at the same time every night.

16. Turn off all electronic devices two hours before bedtime.

Chapter 11

The Power of One

Every strike brings me closer to the next home run.

Babe Ruth, Hall of Fame major league baseball player

From 1915–1919 Babe Ruth pitched for the Boston Red Sox and did so rather well. In 1916 he recorded the lowest ERA and most shutouts in baseball. During his pitching career with the Red Sox, he had a winning percentage of .671, which at the time placed him fifth all time in the record books for career winning percentage. In 1918 a new manager named Ed Barrow was hired. He decided to split Ruth's time between pitching and hitting. His production in both areas subsequently declined.

In 1920 the New York Yankees purchased Ruth for $100,000. Yankee manager Miller Huggins, seeing the tremendous upside and value to the organization, had Ruth focus exclusively on being a hitter for the last 15 years of his career. During that time Ruth led the American League in slugging percentage 13 times, walks 11 times, home runs per at bat 12 times, on base percentage 9 times, and home runs 12 times.

What Huggins did with Ruth is the most mission critical aspect of leadership whether it is leading a baseball team, sales team, or a Fortune 500 company. Great leaders recognize the strengths of their people and let them focus on and play to their strengths. I've found that helping your people discover what I call "the power of one" is the single greatest game changer in terms of both leadership and workplace performance. I define the power of one as the ability to identify and maximize the one thing you do better than anyone else. Leaders who can help their people discover their unique talent and channel it into their work will have unparalleled results.

My passionate belief in this game-changing philosophy stems from my study of strengths-based leadership that I have since implemented in both my coaching and consulting careers. Before I began my consulting career, I spent 12 years as a college lacrosse coach and teacher. Prior to the 2001 season I read Marcus Buckingham's book *Now Discover Your Strengths*. It had a profound impact on the results I achieved as a coach. Utilizing strengths-based coaching and leadership that year my team had a turnaround season. Expanding on that model, the following year my team had a breakthrough season, advancing to the NCAA Final Four and finishing the season ranked third in the national polls. My mantra with my 2001 team was "bring the thing," as in channel the power of your one thing you do better than anyone else.

More important than the outcome of the games was the fact that through strengths-based leadership my players were able to discover the talents that made them unique and consequently maximize their potential. The leadership lesson for me was focusing on what your people can do well is far more powerful than trying to improve what they don't.

Every day leaders outside of sport do to their people precisely what the Red Sox did to Ruth. They play it safe. The primary reason they do so is in an attempt to strike a balance in how they utilize multitalented employees. There are a variety of other reasons managers will play it safe. I like to say that "conservative is the new progressive" right now. In this economy, playing it safe has become the staple of many an organization's diet. Aversion to risk is never more common than in a down economy.

The mistake made is that in an attempt to be a prudent decision maker a leader, like Barrow, fixates only on the most apparent results of a decision. When leaders becomes fixated on the obvious or safe benefits of their personnel decisions, he or she neglects to factor in the downside of those decisions. In the case of Ruth, we need to look no further than the record books to see what Red Sox manager Barrow left on the table in terms of hidden costs. Hits, home runs, and runs batted in to name a few. Many baseball statisticians estimate that had Ruth spent his whole career in the field instead of splitting responsibilities while in Boston he might have hit north of 800 home runs.

Play it safe is also playing not to lose as opposed to playing to win. Playing to win involves the courage to take calculated risks and swift action geared toward your individual and organizational strengths or core competencies. The irony is playing not to lose will never allow you to win. Leaders who play not to lose neglect to see the hidden costs associated with this game plan.

Miller Huggins had the leadership insight and courage to let Babe Ruth discover his power of one by using his strengths exclusively. How are you enabling your people to discover their power of one and operate in their strength zone at work? Helping people discover their unique talent is about seeing them for what they can be, rather than as they currently are and then showing them what they are truly capable of achieving. Helping people to develop the self-awareness to define their unique talent is what provides an organization with the ultimate competitive advantage.

There is an old expression and as cliché as it may seem, I guarantee you it's true in every board room, meeting room, classroom, and locker room anyone has ever set foot in. "They don't care how much you know until they know how much you care." People want to work with a leader who inspires them to be their best and wants to help them achieve their maximum potential. By helping your team members uncover their one unique talent or greatest strength, you're demonstrating to them that you care about them as people, not just as human capital in the workplace.

The leader should both help each team member answer the following question and answer it himself: What is the one thing I do better than anyone else that can help this team or organization be successful?

There are then four sub-questions within this one important question to help bring focus and clarity to the individual's answer.

1. What is needed?
2. What am I good at that I can become great at?
3. What is the one little thing I can I do to differentiate myself that nobody else is willing to do?
4. What should I avoid doing?

A question I have often asked my players both as a group and in individual meetings is: If you are not a goal scorer, how can you help us win games? The purpose of the question is to remind each team member that scoring goals is not the role of every player on the roster. It also gets them thinking about what their one thing can be. What is the other area of play you can potentially dominate? Perhaps the player has excellent field vision and can become the best passer on the team. Another example is that each year regardless of athleticism and scoring ability there would be a starting position on offense for the player who could set the best pick. This was as critical a skill as scoring or passing, so we created a metric to measure it. Pick setting is actually even more significant than goals and assists because without a good pick being set, often the scorer might not get open to receive or shoot the ball. Thus the pick man makes it all possible for the players who score the goal and get credited with the assist.

One of the ancillary benefits of asking the question "What's your power of one?" is it makes each member engage in self-reflection and assess how he best contributes to a team's success. Some players who may traditionally respond to situations in a reactive manner are now taking ownership over this question in a proactive manner. It is requiring personalities who tend to be introverted to now be communicative and take responsibility for bringing their best to the team. When they begin to channel their one thing, they then take ownership over the role and excel at it.

You often hear the media and many coaches refer to certain athletes on the team as "role players." I have always disliked this characterization and felt it minimized or diminished certain player's value to the team. The reality of it is that on my teams every player was a role player; everyone just had different roles. If the first team All-American left the game due to injury or a penalty, the reserve player must be physically and mentally prepared to step in and perform—and in the process know where his role fits in with that of his teammates.

Every leader needs to be able to define what it is that she or he uniquely contributes to the organization and specifically to the role of leader. The answer will reveal a number of things. How does the individual view servant leadership? How does it speak to one's desire to be accountable and enthusiastic? Is the leader's response congruent with past actions? Ideally, the leader's answer should also speak to the core values of the organization.

Coaching Points

- What is your power of one?

- How are you currently leading? Focusing on strengths or playing it safe?

- Reflect for a moment about one of your employees you previously viewed or labeled as average. What is his or her one unique talent you could tailor a role for that would make that person an exceptional performer?

Part IV

HALFTIME

Chapter 12

Halftime Adjustments

How you respond to the challenge in the second half
will determine what you become after the game,
whether you are a winner or a loser.
Lou Holtz, Hall of Fame football coach

This chapter is the midpoint of *The Coach Approach*. Like the midpoint of a lacrosse game, it is halftime. Television analysts love to interview the winning coach after a closely contested game and ask him what adjustments he made at halftime to win the game. If it is a come-from-behind victory, you also often hear the sideline reporter ask a player on the field, "What on earth did the coach say to you guys at halftime to get the team to play so much better in the second half?" Clearly, halftime is a key time for a coach; it's where you really earn your money. You make adjustments based on what is working and what is not. You share information with your team and inspire them. Good coaches, like good business owners, go into the game with a clear game plan, one that accentuates your strengths and minimizes your weaknesses.

Things don't always go according to the game plan. I have coined a term for that. It's called "Life." So when the game plan isn't working to perfection, at halftime the coach will bring the team into the locker room to regroup and adjust a little. Over the years I've found that when it comes to halftime, less is more. Less strategy, less critique, less negativity, just plain less information. You don't want to have your team go into information overload. Then you run the risk of their suffering paralysis by analysis and not being able to execute anything well. So what I do at halftime is get everyone refocused on the one main thing we have to do well to win.

Less is more in the sport of business, too. There are just too many emails, too many phone calls, too many interruptions. We live in a self-created, self-imposed society of information overload. Instead of focusing on that, focus on the one main thing you have to do to get the win. The key to being a peak performer is keeping the main thing the main thing.

Making halftime adjustments in a game is one part art and one part science. Doing it well can yield excellent results. At halftime you have a limited window to perform a number of key tasks. This is a time to examine what's working and what's not. It involves information sharing as well as inspiration sharing. (Note: Leaders, this is not the time to browbeat your team for their first half performance.) The manner you communicate information with your team at halftime needs to be tailored to fit its mind-set. For example, a team locker room at halftime is one of the most intense and emotionally charged environments you will ever communicate in.

In the sport of business, halftime can mean a lot of different things. It can be halfway through the fiscal year, the halfway point in the relationship-building phase as you attempt to turn a prospect into a client, or halfway through the life of a project team. For some executives it may signify the halfway point in their careers or a midlife career change due to corporate restructuring.

There are a number of takeaways business leaders can glean from how coaches handle halftime. Much like companies can create seasons for their business based on peak times in the calendar, leaders can also create halftimes for adjustment and reassessment. The following paragraphs will take you behind the locker room doors and show you how to implement halftimes in your organization.

The first thing I like to do at halftime is review the statistics from the first two quarters. The numbers are meaningful and help quantify performance and measure accountability, but I try not to get emotional about these numbers on game day. I look for a couple telling pieces of evidence from a quick review of the stat sheet. Based on the numbers, were we able to execute our game plan and objectives? Is our performance today congruent with our overall identity? If not, what needs to change? If so, what do we need to keep doing?

The second thing I do at halftime is meet with my staff. During the first five minutes of halftime, we can review the statistics and discuss what we each see going on. Every staff member views the same situation through a very different lens, so it is important to get these varying perspectives out in the open quickly. We have a series of five questions we want each person to consider during the first half. I have listed them in Figure 4.

Questions to Consider at Halftime

What is our top priority? (Is it still the same or does it need to change?)

_____

_____

We are most effective when

_____

_____

We are least effective when

_____

_____

In order to succeed we need to

_____

_____

In order to succeed we need to stop

_____

_____

Figure 4

Meeting briefly as a staff provides team members time to rest, get composed, and communicate amongst themselves without any coaches present. I have found over the years that often the team leaders will take that five-minute window to sort out the very same issues the coaches are discussing. The information is often better received coming from a peer or a team captain than from a member of the coaching staff. This is why I meet with my team captains before I address the team.

After a brief captains' meeting, the next phase of our halftime protocol is addressing the team. Here, our communication usually goes in one of two directions. When things are going well, a lot of the halftime message will be reminders like: "Continue to do what we do." "Focus on fundamentals." "Keep working hard one possession at a time."

When things aren't going well, halftime is spent recovering, retooling our game plan, regrouping, and remotivating. The team needs to realize the game is not over and games are won or lost in the second half regardless of the scoring margin. Unless you are able to re-instill some hope back into your team, it will not matter what adjustments are made, if any. My approach has always been process-oriented, not outcome-oriented. We don't use the W word, "winning," on my teams; we use the E word, "execution." If we execute our process well, the winning takes care of itself.

We take the approach that it is not about what the other team does. We are not competing against the other team nearly as much as we are competing against ourselves to be the best we can be. By taking this approach we really don't have "rivals," we simply play the same opponent each week—a nameless, faceless team. Who they are and what they are doing matters far less than how we are executing. We cannot control the opposition; we can only control our effort and ourselves. Thus, knowing the psychological make-up of your team members is of paramount importance.

In business and in sport you are constantly learning something new about the competition and about the effectiveness of your game plan. Is the second half going to be a comeback situation or a time to utilize your killer instinct and really put the other team away while you are leading?

The best performers in any industry are constantly assessing their performance. Minor day-to-day or "in game" adjustments are constantly occurring, but halftime affords the organization the opportunity to make a bigger momentum shift or modification to the game plan. You have some situations where the right adjustments often prove to be more valuable than the original game plan itself.

You can follow the same halftime plan with your team.

1. Assess and analyze performance to this point.

2. Get observations, statistics, and feedback from your assistants and team members.

3. Decide on the specific tactical adjustments to make based on competition, the market, and your own game plan moving forward.

4. Debrief the team/organization on the competition and make the necessary tactical adjustments.

5. Provide an opportunity for your team to rest and refocus. Then communicate the plan and remotivate your team to move forward.

Coaching Points

- What adjustments can you make to stay ahead of the competition?

- How are you resting, recovering, and refueling in your professional and personal life?

- What needs to take place to remotivate you for the homestretch?

- What is currently working well?

- What are the top two or three things that need to be changed?

Part V

THIRD QUARTER

Chapter 13

Businessmanship

*Sportsmanship for me is when a guy walks off the court
and you really can't tell whether he won or lost,
when he carries himself with pride either way.*
Jim Courier, Former champion professional tennis player

Crazy as it sounds, sometimes a loss is the best thing for you. Losing from time to time provides us with perspective. Winning streaks can inflate the collective and individual egos of a team, which tends to have a negative effect on future preparation, mind-set, and performance. Leaders must invest a great deal of time and energy in not allowing their team to get too low after defeats but even more in not allowing them to get too high after victories. There is an inherent danger in reading your own newspaper clippings.

In the heat of battle, judgment is sometimes clouded and competitive instincts kick into high gear. Unless you have clarified your organizational values, you cannot count on people's judgment alone to carry them during these times. Recently we have seen how a lack of moral compass or "businessmanship" (sportsmanship in business) has resulted in bankruptcies and government bailouts due to corruption, greed, and unethical business decision making. This is proof positive that a desire to win at all costs doesn't necessarily result in a long-term victory and can indeed be very costly. In the corporate setting, losing business sometimes can serve to clarify your organizational values. What are you willing vs. not willing to do to succeed?

For me, the beauty of the sport of lacrosse has always involved the class and sportsmanship exhibited on the field during and after the heat of battle. Lacrosse is one of the few, if not the only, sport where both teams line up to shake hands before and after each game. Upon conclusion of the game just prior to the handshake line, the winning and losing teams alike give a cheer for one another. Winning the conference sportsmanship award has always been an equal priority with winning a conference championship to our teams. I took great pride in my teams always being known as the team that would play hard within the rules for 60 minutes regardless of score and respect the game, officials, opposition, and ourselves. Sportsmanship is more than an act or a value, it is a life skill.

Winning with class and losing with dignity should permeate into every aspect of our lives. It makes a powerful impression on others. There is a mental toughness to sportsmanship. It means being proactive, responding appropriately, not engaging in knee-jerk emotional reactions, embracing challenges, and injecting positive energy into the process without fear of the outcome. Class is an important element to businessmanship. Class involves not sacrificing your values or compromising your integrity just to win business. It also speaks to not reveling in the competition's mistakes or failures.

In the sport of business, winning is defined by increasing market share, return on investment, gaining commitment from a client for additional business, improved profitability, being first to market with a product or idea. What is often left by the wayside is how this end result was achieved. It has been my experience that sportsmanship in all arenas is appreciated more today because it is needed more than ever before.

The sportsmanship model I have used in coaching is apropos for business as well. Jim Thompson, founder of the Positive Coaching Alliance, developed this model. The PCA is an organization I joined several years ago whose mission is to transform the culture of sport to give young athletes the opportunity for a positive, character-building experience. What drew me to this organization and its mission is its goal of culture transformation. When leaders are inheriting an athletic or work team, there is almost always an element of changing the culture that you want to initiate. Usually this is done to facilitate communication and improve the performance of the group.

The PCA employs a mental model that involves three major elements. The third element pertains directly to sportsmanship and honoring the game you are involved in. The acronym ROOTS (Rules, Opponents, Officials, Teammates and Self) is utilized to help reinforce the principles of honor and respecting the game.

These five areas became nonnegotiable for my team's performance and conduct. The concept transcends sport and is applicable in all facets of life; teaching responsibility, accountability, trust and maturity—all qualities that would serve my student-athletes well when they entered the workforce and became husbands and fathers. See Figure 5 for my team definition of ROOTS.

Team Definition of ROOTS

R = Playing with maximum effort and enthusiasm for 60 minutes within the rules of the game.

O = Respect and celebrate our opponents as worthy adversaries regardless of whether they do the same or not. Our opponents make us strive to become better every day.

O = Honor our officials as the third team on the field each

---

game. As we have a job to do, so do they. Trust they will do so to the best of their abilities as we also strive to do the same.

T = Understanding that while there is one vision, there will be many voices. We must trust, support, and commit to one another both on and off the field.

S = Putting the team before self is the ultimate way of respecting and honoring yourself. It is about being a servant leader and developing a culture of servant leadership where service above self is the focus of each team member's actions.

Figure 5

These principles apply to business as well as they apply to sport. How well do you honor your profession and your organization's culture and traditions? How do you respect the rules of the game in your industry?

Your organization's reputation is a core component of its ability to succeed. A lack of integrity in one part of the company or one team member can erode the integrity of an entire organization. There is tremendous value in not only verbalizing your stance on businessmanship but also in writing it down and sharing it with your organization. There are some difficult but revealing questions that will force you to take a long hard look at yourself as you clarify your philosophy on businessmanship.

What are you committed to doing?

What practices do you refuse to engage in?

How do you handle staff members who break the rules?

Have you knowingly or unknowingly created a culture that encourages them to bend the rules?

You must develop your two non-negotiable laws of businessmanship.

To maximize our potential, we will:

_____

_____

Even if it results in losing business or turning down business, we won't:

_____

_____

In coaching it was commonplace to find a lot of recruiters engaging in negative recruiting—bashing the competition in an attempt to gain a competitive advantage over a rival institution. The business world is no different. I made it a point to impress upon my staff and players that we would always take the high road. I would rather lose a particular recruit in the short term than lose my integrity and credibility with coaches and prospects' families in the long term. The reality was if another institution was a better fit for a recruit, then I would tell the family that. Over the years, I found that some competitors remembered this and did the same for me.

The best thing you can do in business is lead with your strengths, demonstrating your values and how you differentiate yourself from others in the industry. When most things are equal, prospective clients will be sufficiently impressed with your transparency and integrity that you will win their business.

Coaching Points

- Am I as gracious at losing new business as I am at winning it?

- Do I give my smaller clients the same level of professionalism and personal attention that I give key accounts?

- Am I conscious not to speak negatively about a competitor?

- From time to time do you find yourself more concerned about commissions and profits than businessmanship and service to the client?

TIME OUT

THANKING YOUR COMPETITORS

There is an inspiring poem that sums up the value of having worthy adversaries in business and in life. I have prominently displayed this poem in our team room and player manuals, I now share this with my consulting clients who often do the same.

I THANK MY COMPETITORS

My competitors do more for me than my friends.

My friends are too polite to point out my weaknesses, but my competitors go to great expense to tell of them.

My competitors are efficient and diligent.

They make me search for ways to improve my products and services.

My competitors would take my business away from me if they could.

This keeps me alert to hold what I have.

If I had no competitors, I would be lazy, incompetent and complacent.

I need the discipline they enforce upon me.

I thank my competitors.

They have been good to me.

God Bless Them All

—Author Unknown

Chapter 14

Greater or Lesser, Never Equal

One thing I believe to the fullest is that if you think and achieve as a team, the individual accolades will take care of themselves. Talent wins games but teamwork and intelligence win championships.

Michael Jordan, NBA Champion and Hall of Famer

A team is never equal to the sum of its parts; it is either greater or lesser. The X-factor that determines whether it is greater or lesser is the organization's ability or inability to cultivate a culture of team synergy and competitive excellence. On the list of teams that exemplify this culture, there is one that stands head and shoulders above all others.

The 1980 U.S. Olympic men's ice hockey team was arguably the greatest team ever assembled. The very reason Coach Herb Brooks' team was successful is the same reason virtually all other all-star teams consistently fail. Most all-star teams are nothing more than a collection of egos too big to fit on the team bus together. We need to look no further than many of the U.S. Olympic basketball teams in recent history. Brooks' hockey team was a thoughtful assembly of selfless players possessing a variety of unique talents that when placed together on the same roster complimented one another nicely. In other words, the coach was wise enough to select the right people and put them in the right roles with the right goals. This concept is at the operational core of team synergy.

Brooks took a lot of heat for not allowing boosters and USOC staff members to have a say in the evaluation and selection process. His reluctance was based on the fact that he knew they would not see the team with the same set of eyes he did. They would be star struck by big names and All-Americans instead of staying focused on a rather simple formula of putting the right people in the right roles with the right goals and rewarding or reinforcing the right behaviors. Effective coaches put their teams in the best position to be successful. Brooks even went so far as to examine the psychological profiles of his players to determine who would work best with others on and off the ice. (He did this well before it became fashionable to do so.) The best business leaders also share this eye for awareness of detail and the nuance of team chemistry.

I continue to be amazed that we are 30-plus years removed from the 1980 Olympics and other teams (and corporations for that matter) haven't figured out this is the formula to follow to build a culture of team synergy and competitive excellence in any industry. The one exception to this generalization may be the New England Patriots. The Patriots organization from top to bottom embraces the team-first mentality of its coach Bill Belichick. It is a philosophy embraced not only by players and coaches but by the ownership as well. There is great clarity at all levels as to the manner in which the team is built.

To put it in academic terms, if teambuilding were a course in school, it would more closely resemble a chemistry course than a math course. The reactions that take place when you combine personalities can mirror the chemical reactions of liquids displaced out of their individual test tubes into a beaker. Combine this with the variable of temperature and the reaction can run a wide range of options from positive to neutral all the way to toxic or in some cases catastrophic.

When building a group into a team, the math never adds up quite like it would on a calculator. It is far more probable that two plus two will equal three than four. Rarely will a team ever equal the sum of its parts, more often due to the "chemical reactions" it will only amount to a total of three. When the leader and the team members are able to put ego aside and work for the good of the team rather than simply on the team, two plus two will exceed four. This is the culture of team synergy and competitive excellence that resides in the DNA of championship teams, figuratively speaking. By aligning core values and selecting individuals with complimentary roles who are willing to sacrifice their own personal ego for the collective success of the group, a leader can transform the culture of his team into a winner.

While organizations all seek to increase productivity, spark innovation, and improve bottom line results, most are also neglecting teambuilding and communication training. At the same time, leadership is frustrated with a lack of results or process improvement during a particular initiative. You cannot innovate and improve results without first improving the attitudes and relationships that so often are the very source of the breakthroughs in great results.

In the organizations I work with, a part of my role as a performance consultant is helping build groups within the company into high performing teams and developing rules of engagement in terms of how the members will function with one another.

In my consulting work, I often ask my clients and their teams to describe the worst team they have ever been on and also the best team they have been a part of. They can quickly point out the characteristics of each of these teams with ease. As a matter of fact, the responses are almost instantaneous. I believe this speaks to the significant impact those characteristics had on the team. While it may be the case that these characteristics are top of mind, at the same time they have difficulty assembling and developing a team to meet the criteria they described as constituting a team of excellence. Criteria such as vision, values, support, accountability, integrity, respect, good listening skills, love, and trust. This difficulty is most often attributed to the fact that the organization does not regularly reflect on how they should go about assembling and building specific teams. Instead, what they have assembled more often is really a group or committee, not a team in the truest sense of the word.

I would like to share with you a phone call I receive, if not every week certainly every month. I have the same conversation virtually every time, just with a different person. A business leader will approach me to ask me to run a teambuilding workshop. Usually he or she wants to do a one-day retreat off-site and inevitably mentions wanting to do a ropes course. My first question is almost always "Why do you want to do this?" The response, like clockwork, usually involves a variation of the statement "Well that's what most companies do? Isn't it? Everybody does a ropes course for teambuilding."

This response represents a cart before the horse approach. So, I follow up by asking the leader to tell me about the company teambuilding program and any other leadership in action planned for the year. "Start at the beginning of the fiscal year and tell me what you have mapped out for each day, each week, each month and each quarter over the course of the year." The response typically is, "I can't share that with you."

The reason, of course, is because the company doesn't have a year-round plan mapped out. Typically it doesn't have ANY plan mapped out. My immediate follow-up question is, "Okay then, you can just share with me last year's plan." At this point the person usually reveals there has never been a year-round plan to build the group into a team. In an attempt to learn what the company believes constitutes teambuilding I ask what it's done (if anything) recently to build its people into a team.

The responses usually range from buying the group lunch once a month to taking them out for happy hour. These are not teambuilding activities; these are just nice gestures. There is a world of difference between nice gestures and teambuilding. It's the same conversation with different individuals every time. The fact of the matter is that this teambuilding retreat conversation they've initiated is an attempted band aid to be put on a group or committee that has yet to become a team of any sort, much less a high-performing team. A lot of times when leaders contact me about teambuilding work, poor teamwork is a symptom, not necessarily the root of the problem. The root of the problem is usually communication problems and a lack of clarity about a common mission.

I remind prospective clients that I can't help them build a team in one day. It would simply be taking their money for a one-day event because teams are not built in one day. I refuse to take a prospective client's money for a one-day activity because teambuilding for one day alone cannot and does not result in any significant permanent change. Some of the questions leaders need to ask as they create a long-term teambuilding program around an event are: What do you want your people to learn? How do you want them to feel? What do you want them to think about when they leave there? And most importantly, how are you going to follow up the next day, next week, next month, and beyond to ensure long-term change in their collective behavior and performance.

If you are not willing to commit to following up with a yearlong process, you are better off not doing a one-day retreat. A one-day event will cause your team to view you for what you are really are—uncommitted and inconsistent. You're better off taking that same amount of money you'd waste on a one-day event and burn it in the fireplace or give your team gift cards to a restaurant. At least then your team would stay warm or be well fed for a day.

During my career as a college coach, building team synergy would be designed into every activity, every day. Everything from in-season practice plans through off-season weight training and everything in between. We even went so far as to incorporate it into individual workouts and meetings when we felt it necessary. While the activities would be diverse in scope, they all shared a common theme. Each year we created a mission or central theme using our team covenants and built everything from conditioning and team meals, to community service projects and team events around that theme. The activities were always designed to reinforce our values in the covenant. An example would be the value of servant leadership, where we created activities designed to cause our team members to think about and engage in always being thoughtful and considerate toward each other, other students, and the greater community as a whole.

Many organizations don't have a teambuilding process like this. They have an idea or they decide to follow a cookie-cutter type recipe such as a trendy fad like "the day at the ropes course" phenomenon. This fails because just as individuals are each unique, so too is each organization. Management and teambuilding fads fail because every organization is different and has different people that make it tick. Fundamentals and sound principles work because they are timeless and can be adapted and tweaked to meet the unique needs of a group. An athletic team wouldn't be successful running precisely the same offense as its competition, especially if it doesn't have the personnel required to run it. Why would a business be any different? You must build your teams within the company in a manner that is congruent with the organization itself.

Teambuilding is not a one-day effort; it is an everyday thing 365 days a year. And if you think you aren't teambuilding when your people are away from the workplace, you are mistaken. A culture of team synergy and competitive excellence never takes a day off. The bottom line is that if teamwork is important to the operation of your business, you need to make developing it a priority in the day-to-day operation of your business.

If you want your team to buy in to the concept of building a culture of team synergy and competitive excellence, you need to incorporate the process into your team's workday, every day. Teambuilding was a daily part of every practice on my lacrosse teams, whether it was putting the team through a brief activity before practice, built into practice through some creative drills or conditioning, or perhaps a community service activity. We made sure the team-first mentality was at the forefront, not merely in the back, of our players' minds. Teambuilding is not a one-day event. It's not a one-week event. It is an all-the-time event.

Coaching Points

- How are you putting your team in the best position to be successful?

- Do you currently have a year-round teambuilding plan?

- How is your teambuilding reflective of and congruent with the values and mission agreed upon by the team?

- Which is a more accurate assessment of your team? 2 + 2 = 3 or 2 + 2 = 5? Why?

Chapter 15

Full Tank Culture

People don't like you for what they see in you but
what you see in them.

Don Meyer,
All-time winningest NCAA men's basketball coach

Employee engagement is currently at an all-time low in the United States and costs companies an estimated $300 billion dollars annually. In this age of improving ROI and profitability, it is ironic that the key to every company stimulating profitability is the very thing that so many organizations neglect: enhancing productivity and employee engagement.

Leadership that focuses solely on tangibles such as finance or information technology will not enhance organizational performance. More often, it is the intangibles that lead to game-changing performance. In corporate America the central intangible is teaching managers how to relate to and coach their teams. We are a society of relationships and, increasingly, a society of social networks. Performance is achieved by developing effective, meaningful relationships between individuals and in teams.

Dr. John Gottman, a marriage and relationship expert, says there is a formula to successful relationships. His research indicates that marriages are significantly more likely to be successful when the interactions between the couple are 5:1, positive to negative. Similarly, Jim Thompson, CEO of the

Positive Coaching Alliance, believes there is a magic ratio of feedback in coaching athletes that is also 5:1, positive to negative.

As a supervisor or leader are you aware of your current ratio? If so, are you near Gottman's 5:1 benchmark? If not, let the charting begin. It is time to take inventory of your interactions and raise your ratio because organizational culture never takes a day off. Furthermore, your team's culture is a reflection of you, and consequently, developing a culture of competitive excellence begins with you. I believe enthusiasm is a force multiplier in any endeavor. Therefore, developing teams with enthusiasm and a culture of excellence is contingent upon your demonstrating these characteristics in word and deed.

Creating a culture of competitive excellence can best be done by engaging in the practice of filling the emotional tanks of your people. This coaching strategy I learned from Jim Thompson, a thought leader in the field of athletic coaching philosophy. The strategy served me so well on the field as a college coach that I began to use it in all the relationships in my life: consultant, professor, husband, and parent. I will show you how to build a full emotional tank culture, and I encourage you to incorporate these strategies beyond the walls of your organization as well.

Just as cars have gas tanks, humans all have emotional tanks that make us run. An employee's emotional tank impacts his or her energy, attitude, and engagement level at work. The needle on the fuel gauge of our emotional tanks moves up and down from interaction to interaction depending on the quality of that interaction. When our emotional tank gauge reads "F," or full, we are high-performing, efficient vehicles. We are present in the moment, enthusiastic, receptive to feedback, and learning, as well as confident and composed. Conversely, when our emotional tank gauge is reading low or on "E," much like a car our mileage and performance suffers.

Every member of your organization has the ability to be a pump or a siphon. Pumps help fill the emotional tanks of their colleagues, and siphons serve to drain others' e-tanks. When we share positive feedback and emotions or pump up someone's e-tank, it has the effect of not only uplifting the recipient but also of fueling our own performance with positive energy and emotions. At the same time, siphons in the workplace are sabotaging their own performance because every time they make tank-draining comments, their focus on the negative impacts them as well.

Is your workplace communication at or close to Gottman's 5:1 ratio benchmark? Ten years ago I recognized mine was not. I noticed during the 2001 lacrosse season that my ratio hovered around 2:1. To consciously improve this ratio, I began carrying five dimes and a penny in my left pocket. After sharing a positive comment with a student-athlete I moved a dime to my right pocket. I did not allow myself to share the penny or the "critique" component of my feedback until I had successfully transferred all five dimes. Over time that year I noticed a marked improvement in communication and coachability in what previously appeared to be uncoachable or "difficult" team members. It's amazing that I didn't recognize the actual "difficult" team member prior to this. After all, I had been looking at him in the mirror every morning.

This was a veteran team and we were playing essentially the same schedule as the year before. Yet in 2001 we were able to reach a new level of performance with a winning season and a 100-point club member. We fell just one game shy of the championship in our conference. To what do you attribute the improvement? I believe there is no doubt my improved ratio and the value of the positive tank fillers accounted for the corresponding improvement in individual and team performance.

While you may not choose to go to the extreme of moving change from pocket to pocket, do not allow your team to operate on a praise deficit. Use your own positive emotional currency to demonstrate to your staff how much you value them in a concrete and well-defined way. Genuine praise and positive feedback are the two least expensive yet undervalued and underutilized tools for recognizing and appreciating the talents of your people. Positive affirmations, positive feedback, a high-five, shared laughter, and being a good listener all serve as "tank fillers" that help meet employees' emotional needs and ultimately fuel better attitudes, teamwork, and performance.

Paul Spiegelman, founder and CEO of Beryl, a call center company in Texas, uses a long-lost art to fill the tanks of his employees—the handwritten letter. On the anniversary of his or her employment, each employee receives a handwritten note from Spiegelman recognizing years of service and contributions to the company as well as significant personal achievements by family members and children. (Inc.com, 2010) Sharing praise verbally is a positive gesture, but putting it in writing as Spiegelman does takes it to a whole new level. Written tank fillers are like fuel injector cleaners for our emotional engines because the person can save the note, refer back to it, and also share it with others. Think of the emotional improvement associated with that!

Filling your teammates' and colleagues' emotional tanks isn't just a nice thing to do for people. In the moment, it is a seemingly little thing that makes a big difference over the course of a day, week, month, quarter, etc. It is powerful fuel that energizes your culture and serves to reward as well as reinforce important contributions team members make to the organization. Additionally, when you are filling emotional tanks, you are also reinforcing and recognizing behaviors you want to see repeated. Coaches like to say, "That which gets recognized gets repeated."

To create a full-tank culture, you need to exemplify the behavior you want to see in your team. The team won't buy it if you don't own it yourself. In other words, if you behave like a siphon, you will never develop a team full of pumps. Among every leader's goals should be modeling the behavior to create a full-tank culture where coworkers fill each other's tanks.

Teamwork and engagement rise to the next level when colleagues work for each other, not simply with each other. Boston Celtics great Bill Russell said it best when analyzing his own performance, "The most important measure of how good a game I played was how much better I'd made teammates play." It's easy to be a tank-filler when things are going well; it's much harder when adversity strikes. Coincidentally, it is also most important to be mindful of filling your teammates' tanks when the chips are down. Winners are at their best when the circumstances are not. Your role is a conscious daily choice, so ask yourself frequently if you are being a pump or a siphon.

How to Use the Full-Tank Culture to Coach Your Team

There are steps to gauging the engagement level of teams before commencing a meeting or project. Amy Nakamoto, executive director of D.C. Scores, a nonprofit located in the nation's capital, has maintaining a full-tank culture as one of her top priorities as a leader. Her initial daily gauge reading of her staff consists of taking note of interactions among staff members, tone of voice, body language, mood, and posture. At the beginning of each interaction with an employee or group of her employees, Nakamoto asks them each to share what their gauge reads (on a scale of 1 to 10, with 10 full and 1 empty).

The rationale is that to best relate to and coach employees, you need to know where they are at that moment. Then you meet them there and tailor your communication to get them to a higher level of engagement. By performing this check, you can adjust the intensity and structure to the level of their tanks. This process is the management equivalent of physicians reading their patients' charts and vital signs while making rounds in the hospital.

How to Use It to Coach Individual Employees

Taking a gauge reading of staff members' emotional tanks also allows you to interact on an individual level more effectively. For example, if in your staff meeting 20 people report their gauges being at or near a ten and two individual's gauges are reading at a two or a three, this quick check-in will let those two members know everyone else's level is high and their work as a group will be tailored to a higher level. You can then invest more time one-on-one with these individuals to elevate their levels during the course of your group's work and the course of the day.

How to Build a Full-Tank Culture

Nakamoto incorporates emotional tank instruction into the on-boarding process for new employees. She explains the purpose and use of the practice to all new hires and has created an in-depth description of the DC Scores e-tank rating system. She explains what each rating feels like all the way up through a ten. Her use of this practice is truly masterful as it serves to teach mindfulness and self-awareness in the workplace as well as sets the proverbial bar high on team members consistently having a full tank. Frequent gauge readings help you teach your staff how to read both themselves and each other better. The benefits are improved teamwork and office dynamics because employees are able to be on the lookout for symptoms of a low tank.

Practice Script

I have listed a practice script for providing tank fillers in the moment. Use this by reflecting back on an activity or contribution by a colleague you recently witnessed in the workplace (the more recent the better).

1. WHO: Person's name.
2. WHAT: What stands out about their performance?
3. WHERE: Location it took place.
4. WHEN: How recently?
5. WHY: 3 to 5 words that best describe his or her positive contribution.
6. HOW: Positive comment as to how this speaks to his or her character or fits his or her strengths. (One sentence)

An example is: "Susan, I appreciate the way you stepped in and helped Lisa put the finishing touches on the marketing materials for the XYZ account this morning. Your insights, selflessness, and teamwork really helped us meet our deadline. It says a lot about you that you put your own work aside for the morning to make sure we executed this to perfection. Thanks."

This process can also be used to fill the emotional tanks of work teams and project teams when the performance is a collective effort.

To maintain your ownership of a full-tank culture I have created a 10-point inspection for you to make over the course of your workday to help ensure you are the model tank filler. See Figure 6.

**FULL-TANK CULTURE:
A DAILY 10-POINT INSPECTION**

1. *"5 by 9 Rule."* I've made 5 deposits in the tanks of others by 9 a.m. today.

2. I've made consistent deposits in the emotional tanks of others throughout the day.

3. I look for the best in others, seeing their strengths before their weaknesses.

4. I make time to listen to the needs of others.

5. I consistently exhibit "infectious enthusiasm."

6. I use humor as a tank-filler.

7. I let my staff know when I catch them doing something well. (Catching them in the act and filling their tank in the moment makes it a shared experience where the praise is genuine and sincere.)

8. I recognize and praise others on their effort rather than outcomes (regardless of business conditions).

9. I have thanked (verbal or written thank-you notes) at least three people today.

10. I utilize a system for regularly charting my magic ratio. (Tally marks on a note pad, moving coins from pocket to pocket, reviewing audio recordings of my meetings, etc.)

Figure 6

Coaching Points

- How are you developing effective, meaningful relationships with colleagues and team members?

- Are you aware of your current ratio? If so, are you near Gottman's 5:1 benchmark?

- How will you go about charting your ratio to take inventory of it?

- *"That which gets recognized gets repeated."* What are the two most important contributions a team member can make that you want to recognize more?

TIME OUT

FULL TANK CULTURE
The Pump vs. The Siphon

A pump is part of the solution. A siphon is part of the problem.

A pump makes plans. A siphon makes excuses.

A pump asks, "How can I help you succeed?" A siphon says, "That's not my problem."

A pump finds opportunity within problems. A siphon finds problems within opportunities.

A pump sees the goal. A siphon sees the goalie.

A pump says, "That will be challenging, but WE can do it." A siphon says, "We can't do that; it's too challenging."

You wake up every morning and have a choice to make. What's it going to be . . .

Pump or Siphon?

Chapter 16

Award Board

*There's nothing greater in the world than when somebody
on the team does something good and everybody gathers around
to pat him on the back.*

Billy Martin, Major league baseball manager

The greatest source of workplace motivation is appreciation. The same holds true in sports. Players feel more fulfilled, satisfied, and assured that they are contributing to team goals when they are recognized for their efforts. Notice I did not say recognized for their achievements or production or results. Many times in the workplace or on a team there are unsung heroes whose work is integral to the success of a team, yet their names do not appear in the box score, much less the headline in the newspaper.

Perhaps the single most powerful motivational strategy we used in my lacrosse program over the years was something we called the "award board." As Hall of Fame basketball coach John Wooden liked to say "It takes ten hands to make a basket;" on a lacrosse team it is double that. While it may take 20 hands to score a goal, only two names appear in the box score: the person scoring the goal and the person who passed him the ball who gets credited with the assist. Yet there were numerous contributors to that end result, for example, our goalie who

119

made a save on the other end of the field to jump-start our offense, the player who may have caused a turnover to create our possession of the ball, the player who set a pick to get the scorer free from his defender, and the list goes on.

Without these seemingly unspectacular efforts, the spectacular goals would not appear on the scoreboard. Therefore it is critical to recognize these efforts publicly. I would often drive the media nuts because when reporters would ask to speak to certain players postgame, I would send them different members of the team. The goalie who made the save that led to our goal would get sent to the postgame interview rather than the person who scored it. The face-off man who got us frequent possession of the ball would appear before the reporters as opposed to the team member with the most points on the day.

I cannot emphasize enough that little things win big games. Seemingly little things make a big difference in business as well. I deliberately use the word "seemingly" because there is perception and then there is reality. The public perception is that these contributions are little things; the internal reality is they are in fact of enormous magnitude.

In its annual employers' survey of 2008, Deloitte Consulting LLP said the number-one employer challenge cited was *"the ability of reward programs to attract, motivate, and retain the talented employees we need to effectively run our organization."*

What are you doing to reward and recognize your people responsible for doing the seemingly little things?

In my lacrosse program we created weekly awards given out at the start of each new week to recognize performance from the prior week. The Positive Coaching Alliance refers to these as targeted symbolic awards. We would not only display the recipient's names on an actual board in the locker room but also on the website, team newsletters, and press releases. Our award board included the following targeted symbolic awards:

- *The black jersey:* Practice player of the week (wears black jersey in practice the following week)
- *The anchor:* Most consistent player (anchor—holds fast, steady, solidly planted)
- *The spike:* Player who does something to build the team without drawing attention to himself (like a railroad spike keeps the track in place and the train on track)
- *The hammer:* Hardest legal hit on game day (Slogan—Be the hammer, not the nail)

These awards were measured both quantitatively and in a very qualitative or subjective way by our coaching staff and players. The coaches would meet along with the team captains and discuss the merits of players' performances to determine who earned recognition. The beauty of these forms of recognition is that they shift the focus away from individual statistics and at the same time reward specific behaviors that contribute to team chemistry and results on the field.

The basic idea is similar to incentive programs in some businesses. It is a way to reward a unit or an individual for performance and meeting certain team goals. Most teams use award decals on the players' helmets. I opted for the award board because I believe it is important for a uniform to be exactly that. Everyone on the same page: looking the same, thinking the same, and playing the same on game day right down to the appearance of the helmet. (Coaches originally modeled the concept of decals after fighter pilots marking their planes with stickers after kills and successful missions.)

There are numerous benefits to creating an effective recognition program: talent retention, better identification of and recognition of your top performers, and enhanced accountability, to name a few. Perhaps more importantly, there is a certain pride that emerges with the introduction of such an incentive program. A healthy internal competition grows as teammates compete and push each other to another level in order to gain the recognition via the award board. Proper recognition also serves to validate a player or employee's contribution and consistent performance at a high level. It is a powerful way for leaders to connect with their team members and drive engagement to the next level. When you are specific with what you recognize and why you are recognizing it, you help form a stronger connection between goals of the organization and result-producing activities team members perform on a daily basis.

Coaching Points

- Coaches like to say what gets recognized and rewarded gets repeated. What positive behaviors are you recognizing?

- How many hands does it take to make a sale or fulfill an order in your company?

- How do you recognize the unsung heroes on your team?

- Can you identify the most critical little thing that wins big games for your team?

TIME OUT
TOP TEN CELEBRATION STRATEGIES

1. *Keep a success journal.* Document three successes by 5 p.m. no matter how small they may seem. These can be personal as well as professional successes. Encourage your staff (and your children) to do the same in their lives.

2. *Involve others.* Encourage colleagues, team members, and employees to huddle briefly at the end of the day to share victories of all sizes with one another. Winning is contagious, so this will boost morale as well as create positive momentum.

3. *Make it fun.* Celebrate wins in a fun way. Announcements over the intercom and email, crazy awards at staff meetings,

4. *Give yourself a shot in the arm.* In order to keep your spirits up in downtimes, review your success journal. It will show you tangible evidence that you are indeed making progress toward your goals.

5. *Vitamins for your mind.* Make it a daily practice to spend a few minutes reading an inspirational story or success quotes, or watching an inspirational video. The best vitamin of all is to watch yourself on video experiencing success.

6. *T.O.M.A.* Also known as top-of-mind awareness. Advertise success to make it top of mind. Post success quotes, signs, and images of success that speak directly to you and your organization's culture in visible, high-traffic areas where you and others will read them. Several great locations are mirrors, doors, computer monitors, water coolers, break room, conference room, and walls at the end of hallways.

7. *Celebrate the grind.* Recognize and take pride in the fact that you work hard and give 110 percent every day. Sustaining your effort and executing your process over time is the number-one key to success. Therefore you need to celebrate the process.

8. *"Expect To Win" mentality.* Develop a mentality within your culture that success comes in all different shapes and sizes. It is expected, and most importantly, celebrating it is mandatory.

9. *Sights and sounds of success.* Focus on positive visualization and self-talk because in order to be successful, you must first look and sound successful to yourself. Remember we are all in sales, and the first sale you make is the one you make to yourself.

10. *Deposits of success.* Provide your team members with deposits in their emotional tanks using recognition, appreciation, and positive feedback.

Chapter 17

Hearing vs. Listening

Communication does not always occur naturally, even among a tight-knit group of individuals. Communication must be taught and practiced in order to bring everyone together as one.

Mike Krzyzewski, Duke University basketball coach

It is the first aspect of communication we learn, the one we use the most, and yet are taught how to do the least: listening. Several years ago, I witnessed a coaching clinic where Dave Pietramala, coach of the 2007 National Champion Johns Hopkins lacrosse team, spoke about his team's level of communication on the field. Specifically, about how his players needed to communicate more with one another on defense.

To facilitate increased communication on game day, he began having the players talk to each other from the moment they walked out the locker room doors on their way to the practice field and continuing through stretching and warm-ups. The players were "required" to talk to one another constantly. All coaches and business leaders understand the importance of communication within their teams, want it, and preach it, but how many actually teach it?

This exercise underscores an important concept on all teams: talking vs. communicating. When you talk, it is a one-way process of sharing information without a response being required from the other party or parties. When you are communicating, it is a two-way process. An exchange of information (both verbal and nonverbal) that mandates a response. I understand Pietramala's goal for his team but believe the process should be tweaked for a better result.

I would rather have communication among my team members than talk. Even with communication there is a distinction between hearing and listening. You may hear someone but are you truly listening? Your response indicates the answer. This prepractice exercise is a great example of teaching communication and getting your people all on the same page. Regardless of industry or task, in order to perform well together you must first communicate well together. You cannot simply tell your staff or team, "You all need to be communicating." You have to teach them how to do it effectively.

Marquette University men's basketball coach Buzz Williams provided a great example of the importance of effective verbal communication when he spoke at a Nike Basketball Clinic. To emphasize the importance of effective communication, he used the example of "If a blind person came to your practice, what would he think of your team?"

His question is a thought-provoking one for leaders of any organization. For teams, what does a successful practice or game sound like? For corporations, what does an effective meeting sound like? What you say is important. How you say it is even more important in determining how it resonates and if it sticks. In both settings I listen for a number of sounds and their qualities, in other words the message within the message. Some key examples of the message within the message that I look for are active listening, questions, answers, affirmations, praise, clapping hands, and moving feet.

What type of sounds are you looking for from your team and employees? Specifically, what do you want to hear from your team members in terms of terminology, praise, and critique? I am careful to listen for certain pronouns, to the point where

I chart the ratio of their presence vs. others. Two key ratios I chart are the ratio of I or Me vs. We and also We or Us vs. They or Them.

Hearing my players' I:We ratio decrease as the preseason moved through the season was always reaffirming to me and a great indicator of developing buy-in. An employee's choice of pronouns can be a telltale clue about that person's buy-in on a project or engagement level in the organization. This choice underscores the importance of listening. The only time you should use the words "I" or "me" is when you are accepting the blame or holding yourself accountable for something. Otherwise you run the risk of being viewed as self-absorbed and not thinking of the team first.

People lacking one of their five senses develop a heightened acuity of their remaining senses. Being the parent of a hard-of-hearing child led to my involvement on the board of a national nonprofit organization for education of the deaf and hard of hearing. My work there has had a profound impact on my view of the communication process as a whole, especially on how I view communication within groups. Armed with this new perspective and fascinated by the question Williams posed, I took his advice to heart and not only employed a blind person to analyze my team's verbal communication levels but also a deaf person to provide insight into my team's nonverbal communication skills.

Williams takes this exercise to the extreme to illustrate his point. He has shown footage of practice minus the video, audio only. Doing so forces his players to only hear practice and emphasizes the importance of effective communication. Williams also dubs practice onto audio-only CDs and listens to them in the car on the way home. After experimenting with this for a season myself, I have made it a best practice in my coaching and encourage my clients to do the same with their business team's meetings.

Mark Twain once said, *"Kindness is the language which the deaf can hear and the blind can see."* I would revise this to read teamwork and kindness. We clearly learn more with our eyes and ears than our mouths.

Consider what a blind person would say about your team's communication with one another if he or she audited a department meeting. What grade would a deaf person give your department's nonverbal communication skills with one another. What does this say about your team chemistry? Your employees engagement level? Morale? Management expert Peter Drucker sums it up best with his statement that "the most important thing in communication is to hear what isn't being said."

There is a big difference between talking and communicating, and there is also a big difference between hearing and listening. Over the years I have placed a premium on eye contact. It is one of the first signs of engagement and part of teaching people how to listen. Whether I am speaking to the team, an assistant coach is instructing the group, or teammates are addressing one another, no one starts talking until they have everyone's eye contact. At the beginning of a conversation, try looking at the person's eyes long enough to make note of what color they are.

Meet with your team, and then stop and ask someone to repeat what she or he heard. Coach Bob Knight used to have a mock timeout and then pass out index cards to his team members so they could write down what they heard. Try doing the same within your organization. Compare the content of the index cards and determine what common themes emerge.

Great leaders are great listeners, and the very best listen for what isn't said as much as for what is said. They ask open-ended questions and effectively utilize a pause to gain additional information from the communicator. According to *Harvard Business Review,* "The number-one criteria for advancement and promotion for professionals is an ability to communicate effectively."

It is not enough to merely say something to your staff as if you are issuing a decree from on high. You must also be a visual, living embodiment of your message. It is essential you lead from the front by example and exhibit the very qualities you want your team to perform. During the 2010 season, New York Jets quarterback Mark Sanchez was watching himself on film and based on the negative body language he saw himself exhibiting decided to create an accountability system. He asked his coaches to issue him small fines every time they saw him slump his shoulders, hang his head after a bad play, or march off the field visibly frustrated.

Psychologists say that over 90 percent of what we communicate is nonverbal. How aware are you of that fact on a daily basis? Many people's actions and words are often incongruent. How present and engaged are you moment to moment in the workplace? To heighten your awareness, consider creating an office body language jar, where you can pay a small fine every time colleagues notice negative nonverbal cues on display by one another. Watch the body language improve quickly!

When my players were in a slump, I would often have them carefully monitor their nonverbal communication. My rationale was that you communicate body language like posture and facial expressions to yourself first and then to the rest of the world. We tend to listen very carefully to what we say to ourselves both verbally and nonverbally. Therefore it is important that we are mindful of our internal communication. Good posture helps you project an air of confidence and increases your credibility. The power of facial expressions cannot be underestimated either. Smiling, for example, is the ultimate sign of welcome and approachability. Research indicates that smiling at people actually activates the reward center in their brain.

Good communication is a competitive advantage on the field as well as in business. The importance of good communication cannot be underestimated. On the field when you are vocal and communicating well, you can get a step ahead of the competition. The ability to communicate what is about to happen before it happens is a competitive advantage in any arena.

Communication also breeds confidence. If you are communicating with teammates on a project and they know you have their back and are ready to help at a moment's notice, their approach to their assignment will have more confidence and zeal. Communication can serve as a re-engagement device. If someone isn't paying attention, verbal cues can be the subtle or not-so-subtle cue to get him or her back on track. Effective communication enables you to catch mistakes before they happen on the field and in the workplace. Communication is the transfer of energy; therefore a workplace filled with communication is a more high-energy environment.

Coaching Points

- How do you listen to your people?

- What does their body language say about their listening to you? Are they hearing problems or solutions? Obstacles or opportunities?

- What does communication sound like and look like in your organization?

- What would a blind person say your staff meetings sound like?

- What would a deaf person say about how your communication looks?

- The best communicators are great storytellers. Are you telling a compelling story or simply regurgitating data? (Make an audio recording of yourself at your next meeting, and listen afterwards.)

Part VI

FOURTH QUARTER

Chapter 18

Deep Practice

On a football team, it's not the strength of the individual players, but it is the strength of the unit and how they all function.

Bill Belichick,
NFL football coach, three-time Super Bowl champion

Disengaged employees cost companies in the United States an estimated $550 billion dollars annually. Causes of disengagement vary, but the most common forms are workplace interruptions and distractions. Human interruptions such as water cooler conversations, extended lunches, or uninvited office guests contribute to the "noise" interfering with workplace performance and productivity. Noise from media, social media, email, voicemail, internet, cell phones, pagers, television, and radio contribute to an atmosphere of disengagement and over time begin to collectively erode the expectations of performance in the workplace.

The concept of multitasking is a myth. In fact the problem of information overload is growing exponentially. In a 2010 study, Basex Inc. determined information overload costs the U.S. economy more than $997 billion dollars and knowledge workers lose close to 25 percent of their day to information overload issues. Given that our society has transitioned from an industrial economy to a service- and knowledge-based one, the issue of information overload has become a significant issue and one of growing concern.

If you are suffering from information overload, in most cases I believe you have made a choice to be a victim. Issues of work–life balance and the 24-7/365 access to technology in our wireless world certainly compound the problem. Why? Quite simply because most people allow it to.

The most successful performers in any arena have an ability to tune out distractions. There is a certain mental toughness that peak performers bring to a job, any job they are doing. Take for example the ability of an NFL quarterback orchestrating a game winning drive in the closing moments of a championship game. Examine the noise he is able to tune out: crowd noise, the opposition, fatigue, pain, the elements, and the scoreboard. I think you would agree your information overload clearly pales in comparison. The value of a focused performer or a focused team cannot be emphasized enough. How do the best accomplish this? It is a matter of focus, and you can do the same in your arena. A focus on your responsibilities not your teammates, your performance not your competition.

The New England Patriots football team is in my professional opinion the gold standard of team synergy and competitive excellence in professional sports. Coach Bill Belichick is a master motivator and consistently brings out the best in his people. His use of trigger phrases to reinforce the organizational core values and cultural expectations are subtle but powerful. And if you are a New England Patriots player, they are in your face every day. Literally. Upon entry to the Patriots practice facility there is a sign on display that reads *"WHEN YOU COME HERE, do your job."* It's a trigger phrase to remind each individual that *your* focus is *your* job and you need to do it every day you're here. A team is never equal to the sum of its parts. It is either greater or lesser, and what determines this is a singular focus. This focus of being in the moment facilitates proper preparation, locker room chemistry, flawless execution, and situational awareness under pressure. Coincidentally, if you polled NFL analysts and coaches on what team best embodies these four characteristics, you would find the New England Patriots at or near the top of everyone's list. Most importantly, these characteristics all breed confidence, which is the precursor of successful performance.

In the postgame press conferences after a win, you will hear Patriot players talk about the team and the quality of their teammates' efforts. After a defeat the sound bite you get is always about the team and its need to practice and prepare more diligently in the upcoming week. Press conferences and media outlets are what the coaching staff would call "noise," and media attention today is clearly information overload. Too often outside expectations and media noise impair performance, both on the field and in business. Filtering information and blocking out noise is a competitive advantage you can't put a price tag on. If the players didn't get the first trigger loud and clear upon entry to the facility, the last thing Patriot players see when they step out of the locker room for the game field is a similar sign with the trigger phrase *"Ignore the noise, manage expectations."* This culture and simple yet consistent messages during Belichick's tenure have become known as The Patriot Way.

You don't need to be a coach to do the same; you just need to be a leader. A leader who understands the value of creating a culture of competitive excellence can achieve similar long-term results through effective coaching to maximize focus, preparation, and execution. The business equivalent of The Patriot Way can be seen in advertising and marketing in the concept of TOMA, or top-of-mind awareness. Top-of-mind awareness is a way to measure how well a brand ranks in a consumer's mind. Great coaches are masters at renting space between their players ears in order to ensure they are thinking about the right things at the right times. They sell the team on their philosophy daily to make it stick.

Business leaders can achieve the same results through two marketing principles: frequency and consistency of the message. You don't stop selling things like the company's mission, organizational priorities, the quality of your product, or the quality of work life once the prospective employee has signed on the dotted line. Like a coach, you are in a constant process of selling and reselling your people on the company, yourself, and your team's goals and objectives. Basketball coaching legend, Don Meyer, uses the metaphor of selling your philosophy daily with a soft rain vs. once or twice a year with a fire hose. The greatest benefit of Meyer's soft rain approach is you can measure buy-in by daily observation. Meyer refers to buy-in as shared ownership and he wants a team of owners not renters.

The concept goes beyond mere "engagement," which might be the most overused human resources buzzword of the new millennium. How do you generate buy-in from team members not just for special projects or companywide initiatives but more importantly for the "do your job" aspect of daily performance. Let's face it, your people can be engaged as renters when participating in special projects and initiatives. Daily performance, or the daily grind as many like to call it, requires appealing to your people on a deeper level. I believe, like Coach Belichick, that you must recruit people with pride and then appeal to their pride. There also needs to be an atmosphere of positive peer pressure within the locker room for teammates to be accountable to one another for the quality of their daily efforts. What prompts and triggers are utilized to reinforce the culture and ethos of your department or organization?

As a method of reinforcing our focus on daily improvement and effort, just prior to the start of the season over the holiday break I would mail a letter to team members along with a postage-paid return envelope. Inside the mailing was what we called our "commitment card." It wasn't enough for my players to sign their letter of intent when they committed to attending the college their senior year in high school. Quite simply, there's nothing top of mind about signing a letter of intent. The team needed reminders of our purpose, their role, and the expectations of performance. I felt there needed to be a renewal of purpose at the start of each season. This renewal of purpose was located on one side of the card they would sign and mail back. I guess you could call it a letter of intentionality. When the players returned to campus, we would hold individual meetings in the preseason and discuss what we needed in order to achieve our goals as a team. I would also have each player come up with a trigger word or phrase to represent his focus as a member of the team. Each player and coach would write his word or phrase on the back of his commitment card and then visibly display it on his locker. This enabled everyone to not only hold others accountable but also to coach one another on how to best focus and help the team.

I continue to do this myself and in the organizations I consult. A frequent trigger word I use is "balance." I spend a lot of time in travel consulting and speaking. When I'm not on the road, I invest a lot of time in my writing. The schedule can be exhausting at times. How do you juggle a crazy schedule and maintain physical health, mental health, and healthy family relationships? Balance. Balance to me is about successfully balancing work time with family time as well as rest time. I know that it takes balance in all areas in order to enjoy success in any one of those areas.

I encourage you to do as my teams and clients do. Take an index card, engage in some self-reflection, and then write down the trigger words or phrase that will help give you the right focus to perform at a consistently high level. Share this word with the people closest to you at home and at work. They will be your best accountability partners. Then post this index card in a strategic location where you will view it often over the course of your day. (Think top-of-mind awareness.) Locations

I recommend are on your desk, above your monitor, on the office door or wall, and on your mirror at home. Seeing this card will help you maintain your focus.

While having trigger words is an effective strategy for you as an individual, imagine the difference it could make if you shared them with your team, whether that team is your family, co-workers, or employees. I have been doing this with my teams for years, do it myself, and teach the athletes and executives I coach to do the same.

Coaching Points

- How do you go about facilitating the focus of your people?
- What are the triggers for performance in your organization?
- How are you "soft raining" (marketing, advertising and selling) your people on what is important?
- What's the ratio of owners to renters on your team?
- What sort of noise must you ignore inside and outside the walls of your organization?

Chapter 19

Little Things Win Big Games

It's the little things that make the big things possible.
Only close attention to the fine details of any operation
makes the operation first class.
John Willard Marriott,
American entrepreneur and founder of Marriott Corporation

In sport and business, I have found it is the little things that make the biggest difference. I attribute winning close games to having an eye for detail and being a stickler for making sure the little things are done right. The team that does the little things right and makes the fewest mistakes will emerge victorious. In 2002 my team won six one-goal games en route to an NCAA Final Four appearance. A loss in any of those one-goal games would have knocked us out of contention on our road to the Final Four. It was the little things that enabled us to win each of these games.

Ironically, it was the little things that kept us from winning our National Semifinal game and advancing to the championship game. Specifically, in a 11-7 loss to the eventual national champions, Limestone College, we missed four goals from point-blank range because our player on the crease elected to catch the pass and switch hands before shooting. The seemingly little act of switching hands allowed the defense time to close on him and check his stick while also affording the goaltender additional reaction time on the shots. Over the years since then whenever a player or client questions the value of little things, I share this story. The difference between a potential national championship and nothing is a matter of fractions of a second or inches. The same difference exists in business when it comes to reaction to the market or a competitor. Pay attention to the little things.

The little things also pay big dividends in recruiting and client acquisition. Little things like simply being a person of your word, expressing genuine appreciation, and being kind. I am reminded of a recruiting trip Coach Paul "Bear" Bryant once described during his first year at the University of Alabama.

I had just been named the new head coach at Alabama and was off in my old car down in South Alabama recruiting a prospect who was supposed to have been a pretty good player, and I was having trouble finding the place.

Getting hungry, I spied an old cinderblock building with a small sign out front that simply said "Restaurant." I pull up, go in, and every head in the place turns to stare at me. Seems I'm the only white fella in the place. But the food smelled good, so I skip a table and go up to a cement bar and sit. A big ole man in a t-shirt and cap comes over and says, "What do you need?"

I told him I needed lunch and what did they have today? He says, "You probably won't like it here. Today we're having chitlins, collard greens and black-eyed peas with cornbread. I'll bet you don't even know what chitlins are, do you?" (small intestines of hogs prepared as food in the deep South) I looked him square in the eye and said, "I'm from Arkansas and I've probably eaten a mile of them. Sounds like I'm in the right place."

They all smiled as he left to serve me up a big plate. When he comes back he says, "You ain't from around here then?" I explain I'm the new football coach up in Tuscaloosa at the University and I'm here to find whatever that boy's name was, and he says, "Yeah I've heard of him, he's supposed to be pretty good." And he gives me directions to the school so I can meet him and his coach.

As I'm paying up to leave, I remember my manners and leave a tip, not too big to be flashy, but a good one, and he told me lunch was on him, but I told him for a lunch that good, I felt I should pay. The big man asked me if I had a photograph or something he could hang up to show I'd been there. I was so new that I didn't have any yet. It really wasn't that big a thing back then to be asked for, but I took a napkin and wrote his name and address on it and told him I'd get him one.

I met the kid I was looking for later that afternoon and I don't remember his name, but do remember I didn't think much of him when I met him. I had wasted a day, or so I thought. When I got back to Tuscaloosa late that night, I took that napkin from my shirt pocket and put it under my keys so I wouldn't forget it. Back then I was excited that anybody would want a picture of me. The next day we found a picture and I wrote on it, "Thanks for the best lunch I've ever had."

Now let's go a whole buncha years down the road. Now we have black players at Alabama and I'm back down in that part of the country scouting an offensive lineman we sure needed. Y'all remember, (and I forget the name, but it's not important to the story), well anyway, he's got two friends going to Auburn and he tells me he's got his heart set on Auburn too, so I leave empty handed and go on to see some others while I'm down there.

Two days later, I'm in my office in Tuscaloosa and the phone rings and it's this kid who just turned me down, and he says, "Coach, do you still want me at Alabama?" And I said, "Yes I sure do." And he says OK, he'll come. And I say, "Well son, what changed your mind?" And he said, "When my grandpa found out that I had a chance to play for you and said no, he pitched a fit and told me I wasn't going nowhere but Alabama, and wasn't playing for nobody but you. He thinks a lot of you and has ever since y'all met."

Well, I didn't know his granddad from Adam's housecat so I asked him who his granddaddy was and he said, "You probably don't remember him, but you ate in his restaurant your first year at Alabama and you sent him a picture that he's had hung in that place ever since. That picture's his pride and joy and he still tells everybody about the day that Bear Bryant came in and had chitlins with him . . . "

"My grandpa said that when you left there, he never expected you to remember him or to send him that picture, but you kept your word to him and to Grandpa, that's everything. He said you could teach me more than football and I had to play for a man like you, so I guess I'm going to."

I was floored. But I learned that the lessons my mama taught me were always right. It don't cost nuthin' to be nice. It don't cost nuthin' to do the right thing most of the time, and it costs a lot to lose your good name by breaking your word to someone.

When I went back to sign that boy, I looked up his Grandpa and he's still running that place, but it looks a lot better now. And he didn't have chitlins that day, but he had some ribs that would make Dreamland proud. I made sure I posed for a lot of pictures; and don't think I didn't leave some new ones for him, too, along with a signed football.

I made it clear to all my assistants to keep this story and these lessons in mind when they're out on the road. If you remember anything else from me, remember this. It really doesn't cost anything to be nice, and the rewards can be unimaginable.

This is a story I shared with assistant coaches and my student-athletes to remind them that the little things you do can one day make a big difference for you down the road. For

Coach Bryant the seemingly little things he did made a big difference in helping him land an important recruit. For you, seemingly little things may make a big difference in signing a major account, recruiting a prospective employee, securing an investor, or perhaps making a positive impression on a future employer.

It is a story I continue to share today with my clients and my speaking audiences because it is a story of *The Coach Approach*. It is a message of consistency, little things, attention to detail, and branding yourself or your product. I define a brand as a promise, a promise you make to consumers and potential consumers of your brand. If you want clients or prospective clients to believe you are a first-class organization or team, you as a leader need to engage in flawless execution while treating them in a first-class manner. Consistency of effort in a lot of little things adds up to success in big things.

Coaching Points

- Are you a detail-oriented leader?
- If yes, what little things are you guilty of overlooking?

  If not, who on your team or in another area of the organization can you ask to assist you in maintaining an eye on the little things?
- Think of a time you "missed four point-blank shots." How can you improve your team's execution?
- Like Coach Bryant, through your integrity how do you separate yourself from your competition?
- What is the promise of your brand? Why?

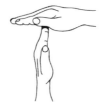

TIME OUT

THE FINAL FOUR PEAK
PERFORMANCE STRATEGIES

1. *High Fives.* The number-one workplace motivator is appreciation. (If you're wondering, money ranks number three.) Provide your people with frequent, specific, and genuine appreciation by recognizing their success and contributions, both small and large. Little things make a big difference. Send a handwritten note. Invest 20 minutes at the beginning or end of your day to do check-ins one by one with your team members. Think of it as a drive-by-shooting of positive feedback.

2. *Feed and Water Daily.* Annual reviews are almost worthless in today's day and age. The reason people don't improve after the annual review and resulting "performance improvement plan" is the feedback and positive reinforcement is far too infrequent. Imagine if you only fed and watered the plant in your office once or twice a year. How would it look? Would it even survive, much less grow? Coaches provide their athletes with constant feedback, not just at the end of the season. It goes beyond day by day, their feedback is play by play. Remember, if we're not green and growing, it means we're ripe and dying.

3. *Laser Focus.* Like the New England Patriots, you can create a process to allow your people to ignore the noise and manage expectations. Resist the urge to expect immediate responses to emails, voicemails, texts, etc. All this does is create mental clutter or noise. The ability to be present in the moment and concentrate for a designated period of time is essential to set the stage for quality performance. Value quality over quantity. Research shows the best coaches get far greater results from what we call "deep practice," shorter, focused, intense practice sessions rather than long, drawn-out ones. Think of focus as a muscle, not a skill. Start small and build it up over time.

4. *Work Like A Midfielder.* Clients often tell me their workdays feel as if they are running on a treadmill. They are constantly moving from meeting to meeting, putting out fires. My advice is to ditch the treadmill and act like a lacrosse midfielder. Think of the workday as a series of shifts. What does a midfielder do? Before the game he visualizes successfully running the field transitioning from defense to offense. He then performs the actual shifts by giving maximum effort in a short, focused burst and afterwards he takes time to rest, recover, refocus, and refuel before the next shift.

Chapter 20

From Adversity to Advantage

Never let what you cannot do interfere with what you can do.
Anthony Robles,
NCAA champion wrestler (born with one leg)

There is a wonderful story about a blind golfer named Tom Sullivan who met professional golf legend Arnold Palmer while Palmer was making an appearance at a tournament for blind golfers in the south many years ago. Sullivan had won this particular tournament on numerous occasions and in their conversation, Palmer asked him how he golfed so well without vision. He explained to Palmer that he would send his caddy out ahead of him to hold a bell directly above the hole and ring it so he could determine the distance and position. Then he would hit the ball to the hole. When Palmer asked him how well that strategy worked, Sullivan responded, "It works so well I bet I could beat you." Palmer laughed it off and told him he respected his abilities as a golfer but there was no way Sullivan could beat him. Not willing to take no for an answer, Sullivan responded that just to make it interesting he would bet $10,000 that he could beat Palmer. Palmer accepted the challenge stating, "Fine, let's play. What time do you want to tee off?" Sullivan replied, "Midnight tonight."

This is turning adversity to advantage. While you may not be Tom Sullivan and your competition isn't Arnold Palmer, maybe he may be the Arnold Palmer of your industry. You, too, can shift your perspective on competing at what you may perceive as a disadvantage and thereby turn the tables on your competition.

If there is one thing I have learned as a coach, it is that the very strength an individual or team possesses can often also be a weakness. Similarly, behind every weakness there is a strength. The key to understanding both of these concepts is in the eyes. Many times professionals are blind to innovative ways to compete. Why? Usually it's not because they lack the mental bandwidth to innovate. Rather, it's because they tend to be too busy cursing the perceived darkness of their situation to view the situation from a positive viewpoint. It takes a unique perspective to identify and exploit an opponent's weakness or properly leverage a particular strength your organization possesses. Much like Tom Sullivan, your vision should not focus on what you lack. I refer to this as creating your "streakness," that is, turning a perceived weakness into a strength or turning adversity to advantage. This is where coaching can have a game-changing impact. Good coaches see players not as they are, rather as they can become, and the great coaches help those players see themselves for what they can be.

While Tom Sullivan's story may be the greatest case of streakness in sports, the most outstanding story of streakness I have ever encountered was by a small business owner in paradise. What would you say and do if the roof collapsed on your businesses, literally? I'm pretty sure "mahalo" wouldn't be one of the first words to come out of your mouth. I ask this question because during a trip to Hawaii, I heard about the most fascinating and inspiring story of turning adversity to advantage and of entrepreneurial resilience.

On September 11, 1992, Paradise Sportswear, a small mom-and-pop T-shirt business on the Hawaiian island of Kauai, was dealt a seemingly devastating blow. Hurricane Iniki, a category 5 storm, overtook the island, destroying almost everything in its path. That destruction included the Paradise Sportswear warehouse and printing facility, as well as its inventory. After the storm, the owners arrived at their building to find the roof caved in and the entire facility flooded with Kauai red clay and water. For those not familiar with the red clay of Kauai, imagine for a moment your home being built on a bed of permanent ink. The Kauaian clay is actually red volcanic soil and is everywhere on the island. The clay is infamous for staining anything and everything it touches. It is the reason Kauaians always remove their shoes before entering their homes.

Knowing the powerful staining property of the clay, the business owner thought all was lost. With bankruptcy looming, out of desperation he decided to try to clean the inventory on the outside chance he could remove some of the clay from the fabric and salvage part of his inventory. The repeated attempts to salvage the many cases of stained white t-shirts failed miserably, and it appeared bankruptcy was unavoidable.

When his efforts were fruitless, the owner decided to attempt to use the red clay to finish the job, completely dying the shirts a consistent color. Despite his wife and his business partner advising against it, he felt there was literally nothing to lose. The shirts were dyed in washing machines filled with red clay and named dirt shirts. One of the most amazing aspects of this "innovention" (one part invention and one part innovation) was that the chemical properties of the red clay made the laundered cotton t-shirts velvety soft and smooth.

A day later, he sold the shirts from a booth in Poipu Beach, and the product was met with a great response. The locals bought up his entire inventory on the first day! The owner-turned-innovator had to return to his facility to produce more overnight. Born of a disaster, from that day forward the concept of The Red Dirt Shirt took on a life of its own and has since become the single most desired tourist souvenir from the island.

I heard about this tremendous success story from a local executive during a trip to Hawaii. Paradise Sportswear's discovery led me to thinking about how we approach business problems and other "collapses" in our lives.

One of the *World English Dictionary* definitions of collapse is "to break down or fall down from lack of strength." Collapses in business can take a variety of forms: financial, physical, or emotional, to name a few. Each poses unique problems, and we can become blinded by our problems, which channels our focus in a negative direction. Negative thought patterns often become self-fulfilling, and the resulting tailspin is difficult to self-correct. Look no further than the recent collapse of several major brands: Circuit City, Oldsmobile, and Borders. As sales fell, they lost touch with exactly what their customers wanted and why they were loyal. Then they did not innovate to adjust to the market. They just simply couldn't get out of their own way.

While a physical collapse is not what led to the demise of these brands, they did suffer from an inability or unwillingness to change and evolve in times of trouble and uncertainty. The takeaway here is that in order to maintain forward progress you need to be able to separate collapses such as a roof, a business concept, a product, or a system within your business from your actual self. If business professionals learned to handle defeat the way elite athletes do, improved results would come quicker and with more consistency. Which in this economy is what we are all seeking, isn't it?

Your ability to maintain forward progress and positive mind-set will increase dramatically by embracing two concepts:

1. *Detachment.* Know the difference between an outcome and an identity. Your identity is not defined by the outcome of an event. Your identity is the sum total of who you are, your unique talents, core values, and outlook on life. For athletes, a loss is merely an event that took place on one day. It does not label them a "loser." The loss is viewed as feedback received and in turn corrections are made for the future. That loss is then put out of mind. The event (loss) did not define them; they defined the event. Failure is merely feedback, and used correctly feedback becomes the breakfast of champions.

2. *Belief.* Maintain the belief that problems are solutions in disguise. Often within our greatest challenges lie our greatest opportunities. Underdog teams understand this concept better than anyone. They are often the only people in the arena who believe they can win, and that is just fine with them. They are also smart enough to know their viewpoint on performance is the only one that matters. A team's belief is essentially shared faith and confidence. Time and time again we see belief trump talent and size in every arena. Why? Because belief allows you to compete without fear. There is no pressure when you have belief. This allows you to stay focused in the moment and be in the zone. You hear the term "playing loose" used a lot in sports. By having belief, you can play loose in the sport of business, which will help you uncover opportunities not visible to many. The owner of Paradise Sportswear found a way to play loose and create opportunity.

The word "crisis" in Chinese means death and rebirth. Through crisis what began as just another sportswear business died and a brand synonymous with Kauai was reborn. Advantage is born of adversity for all of us. The Paradise Sportswear advantage was developed with zero financial capital; intellectual capital was the funding source. Yours can be, too.

Achievement rarely comes without enormous hardships. These are the private victories that are played out over and over again long before the public ever gets to see the individual succeed. Turning adversity to advantage is a conscious decision. It involves a significant element of mental toughness and introspection. Mental toughness is a skill, not a talent. It is learned and developed. It is a process of using your mind to gain the most from your abilities. Finding a strategy or ability to work to your advantage as an underdog can be viewed as a "talent equalizer."

Coaching Points

- What would you have done in Paradise Sportswear's situation? Simply call the insurance adjuster, or call upon your grey matter and imagination? How will your business be reborn in times of crisis?

- What is your Red Dirt Shirt? Examine a current business issue you are dealing with. Like the red clay was to Paradise Sportswear, can the problem itself somehow be the very solution for you?

- What is the number-one way you can create your own talent equalizer by turning adversity to advantage in your industry?

Chapter 21

The Big Mo'

As any athlete knows, momentum is the most unstoppable force in sports. The only way to stop it is if you get in your own way, start making stupid mistakes or stop believing in yourself.

Rocco Mediate, Professional golfer

Momentum is one of the most commonly referred to and least understood phenomena in business and in sports. Positive momentum can enhance your ability to thrive rather than just survive, both professionally and athletically. It is not "mojo" or magic, rather you can manufacture your own momentum and as a result bring about greater productivity, profitability, teamwork, and motivation.

My first instinct was to make this chapter on momentum third words long—Perception is reality. While this description alone doesn't bring clarity to the concept, after reading the chapter you will see that it does in essence sum up momentum. In the sports world, psychological momentum can be defined as the perception that a team or individual athlete is advancing to victory. In a game these "advances" tend to be defined by points scored or scoring margin; in a race it might be defined by separation from the pack by time and distance. A more technical definition in the *Journal of Sport and Exercise Psychology* defines psychological momentum as positive or negative change in cognition, affect, physiology, and behavior caused by an event or series of events that will result in a shift in performance outcome. It is this definition that led me to my three-word synopsis of momentum—Perception is reality.

Haven't we all experienced momentum at one point or another either in sports or in our professional endeavors? Perhaps you have experienced this during a round of golf where you hit a great tee shot down the center of the fairway that eliminated any nervous energy you previously had. This then led to a fabulous approach shot onto the green and a seemingly easy putt to get you under par for the hole. You quickly began to feel supremely confident as you approached the next tee, and the next, and so on. Before you know it, you had one of your best rounds ever. Professionally, maybe it was your all-time best quarter of business that started with a presentation that landed you a seven-figure client. This account, and your resulting confidence, led to referrals netting you three or four clients of similar stature each month. Next thing you know, the phone is ringing off the hook, and you practically can't keep up with the proposals that are leading to more new contracts.

It has been my experience that these things don't happen by accident. Success leaves clues. The problem is most people do not reflect on their performance enough to become aware of exactly what they did to bring about this success and how they can duplicate it. The reason success was enjoyed and repeated in the situations highlighted above is perception. Typically events dictate our perceptions and as a result our response as well. In other words, an event or outcome determined your feelings and thoughts, and these factors then determined your subsequent response or performance. Peak performers strategically take advantage of these positive events and also take steps to eliminate perceptions from negative events. (See success rituals in Chapter 9.)

Momentum packs a lot of performance power because it has a direct effect on our self-efficacy or our belief in our own ability to successfully perform a task or activity. Efficacy often drives success. Positive momentum shifts can also be referred to as "efficacy shifts" in that when an individual perceives performance going well, he gains a greater sense of confidence, control, energy, and motivation. You literally feel yourself playing at a higher level and feeling to a certain extent unbeatable. This place you are sometimes able to go to in your mind is what makes the best of the best precisely that. They don't lease this space in their mind; they own it and find a way to live there consistently.

Because it is based on perception, to a large extent momentum is under our control because as human beings we have a unique ability to control our perceptions. We do this employing several methods: through self-talk, visualization, and our physical behaviors. How do we go about manufacturing momentum? It is simply a matter of systematic effort over time. Notice I did not use the term "easy." Most keys to victory are not elaborate plans, they are simple fundamentals. Simple, however, is not always easy. It is clear and concise but requires discipline and execution.

Successful organizations, like successful teams, are built over time. It is a process of incrementalism, which involves a series of small steps executed consistently over time. When viewed purely in isolation, these steps may not appear significant, but they have a cumulative effect. When you add them up, these daily sustained efforts build into massive success. I have mentioned it before and cannot emphasize it enough . . . little things win big games. More specifically in the case of the big mo', little things add up to create big wins because together they gather momentum.

I often use the example of training for a marathon as a metaphor for business. I do this for two reasons: I am a runner, and distance training is a long-term process requiring discipline and sustained effort. When your body responds in a positive way to exercise, so does your mind and self-esteem. You feel a sense of accomplishment, and it becomes contagious, expanding your vision of what you strive to accomplish and the type of person you can become. You begin to feel more confidence in accomplishing things in other areas of your life. Similarly, when you subject your body to training that has a debilitating or negative effect on you, this feeling will also have a damaging performance effect on other areas of your life.

Creating Momentum

Small daily progress is usually better than trying to take bigger less frequent steps. I like to explain this using a simple mathematical formula: $F > D$, or frequency is greater than duration. In other words, doing a little a lot holds greater value than doing a lot a little. By taking frequent smaller actions, you not only create successful habits but also those small victories or incremental successes that are critical in gathering momentum. This strategy is a lot like training to run a marathon. Compare the training habits of two different runners, one who adheres to a systematic daily training schedule and one who trains occasionally but thinks he or she can make up for the skipped days by running a greater distance with greater intensity. One runner is building momentum for success; the other is cooking up a recipe for failure.

By doing a little a lot (small daily training), the successful runner is building mass, and the consistent daily effort sustained over time creates velocity. The key phrase is "over time." The same can be done in business. Consistent execution of the right efforts daily over time will enable you to manufacture momentum.

There are several factors that strongly influence momentum. The beauty of these factors is that they are directly under your control: process, focus, goals, and consistency.

Process

Consistent performance of the right activities breeds momentum. Implementing and utilizing a process or system for your day-to-day performance breeds consistency. I cannot tell you what one process will be most effective for you as a leader, but I can tell you that without a process you will not be effective at all. I encourage many of my clients to work in terms of themes. Themes can be any designated block of time. It can be a theme for an entire day, such as my theme for "Media and Marketing Mondays," or a theme for a portion of the day, such as devoting Thursday afternoons to planning and scheduling for the upcoming weeks. Working in themes allows you to maintain your focus on one area for an extended period of time. You are working on activities with similar language, types of tasks, and in some cases shared responsibilities with teammates assigned to the same project.

Within any process there must exist goals and a plan to realize them. When you are moving toward a goal and making measurable progress, your perceptions change. As a result of the progress, you will feel increased motivation, higher energy levels, and a stronger sense of purpose and control of the process. This is a primary purpose of incorporating the power of rituals into your daily life. Rituals become a foundational element of your process or system and also serve to prime the pump for peak performance.

Focus

The value of momentum should not be underestimated as the great philosopher Sun Tzu said, *"The value of time, that is being a little ahead of your opponent, often provides greater advantage than superior numbers or greater resources."* How do we gain this advantage of time? Is getting a little ahead achieved merely by working harder or faster? No, the advantage lies in the ability to be here now—to focus on the present without distraction. Many people attribute their lack of focus to the fact that "It is just the way I am." In reality, enhanced focus and concentration can be taught and developed in anyone.

I was introduced to this concept in graduate school during my doctoral course work in sport psychology at Temple University. Our bodies have automatic attention regulators, and people all have different attentional styles. Peak performers excel in part because they have trained themselves to filter, regulate, and direct their attention and awareness to the right things at the right times. My professor Dr. Michael Sachs put us through an exercise called a "concentration grid" in order to prove to us that concentration can be developed through practice. Each day for a week we were given a worksheet with a 10 × 10 grid containing 100 randomly placed numbers starting at zero. We were given one minute to cross out as many numbers as possible in sequence. At the end of the minute we had to add up the number of sequential digits we were able to cross out. At the end of the week we were able to look back and see our scores improve. Improve from a starting point in the single digits to the teens and twenties. The purpose was to demonstrate to us that there will be distractions and lapses in concentration but by consciously practicing being present in the moment and having a system or strategy you can learn to refocus and minimize lapses. It's an activity I continue to use myself and with clients. There is a carryover effect when you are able to eliminate mental clutter and distraction during the concentration grid exercise. Clients report an enhanced ability to stay present in the moment during work-related activities and to eliminate distractions.

Goals

All activities are not created equal, and activity alone does not equal positive momentum. If you are moving toward things you don't really want, you are not creating positive momentum.

Quite the contrary, moving in the wrong direction creates negative momentum. You may be getting a lot of things done, but if it doesn't move you toward your goal, you are creating negative momentum. For example, if you are scheduling more and more meetings with prospective clients yet are not doing your due diligence in research and pre-approach or not following up consistently, activity in this direction is creating negative momentum. We should audit our daily actions to determine if each of them is moving us toward or away from our goals and objectives. Action toward specific results generates momentum. With this in mind, it is important to constantly examine if you are making progress in the right activities. It is mission critical that you keep your goals top of mind. As part of this self-assessment process, there are three key questions you need to consider every day:

1. What direction are you headed vs. what direction do you want to be headed?

2. What could you be doing differently to play at a higher level?

3. What will the destination look like when you arrive?

Self-awareness about what you are truly passionate about and the ability to merge your passion with your core competencies will greatly facilitate momentum. These are our greatest sources of energy. Simply put, passion is an emotion, and emotion creates motion.

Consistency

How can you ensure you are consistently following your process and implementing the right activities? Sometimes it is not a matter of you and you alone ensuring you do so. Having a coach as an accountability partner can help keep you on track better than you can yourself. A coach can hold you accountable to the goals and standards you have set for yourself or your team and help monitor the consistency of your efforts. Consistency facilitates momentum. Consistent sustained effort can be a game changer for the simple reason that it keeps you on track, moving in the right direction toward your goals. As discussed in Chapter 10, research indicates visible daily progress toward your goals is the top workplace motivator. Daily progress is a momentum builder because you are accumulating successes that will build upon one another. Momentum isn't always huge and fast-moving, sometimes the pace of your Mo' will vary. The point is to begin manufacturing it. When performed correctly, it will have a snowball effect.

Maintaining Momentum

The scientific formula for momentum by Sir Isaac Newton is something you can apply to any aspect of your life for better results.

$$M \times V = P$$

$$\text{Mass (m)} \times \text{Velocity (v)} = \text{Momentum (P)}$$

Essentially what Newton is stating is that more you combine the size and the speed of some object, the more difficult it becomes to stop. Think of the mass as your business and the velocity as your activities to move you toward your goal. By increasing either variable (mass or velocity), you can increase your momentum.

Newton's first law says, "An object in motion will not change its velocity unless an unbalanced force acts upon it." This is the benefit of momentum: once you get it going, it becomes easier to keep it going. We see this all the time in sports with a player on a scoring streak who just can't seem to be stopped and in business with the sales professional who is on a roll, moving from one sale to the next and the next. The reason for this is that motion creates action, and with the right actions come results. With results comes increased confidence, and the process self-perpetuates.

Momentum in Action

Perhaps the greatest story of business momentum in the United States is FedEx. Founded in 1973 as Federal Express, on its first night of overnight operations, the company delivered just 186 packages to 25 cities. Six years later in 1979, the company created a state-of-the-art computer system to manage everything in its operation from shipments, drivers, and packages to vehicles and weather, all in real time. It followed this up in 1985 by introducing bar coding to the ground freight industry. In its tenth year of business, Federal Express became the first U.S. company to reach revenues of $1 billion without experiencing a merger or making an acquisition. Another ten years after that milestone, FedEx reached $1 billion again, only this time it was $1 billion in annual revenue for its ground transportation division alone.

Now, nearly 40 years after its founding, the organization is known as FedEx and makes over 7 million shipments a day all over the globe. The FedEx operating strategy is a three-pronged approach. Within it you can see its keen awareness of process, focus, goals, and consistency.

- *Compete collectively* by standing as one brand worldwide and speaking with one voice.

- *Operate independently* by focusing on our independent networks to meet distinct customer needs.

- *Manage collaboratively* by working together to sustain loyal relationships with our workforce, customers, and investors.

The evolution of the organization and its strategy accounts for all four of the aspects of creating momentum I have highlighted. Its focus on innovation has enabled it to evolve its process while continuing to focus on the goal of overnight delivery. Its spectacular industry track record and guarantee of overnight delivery continues to underscore its consistency of performance.

FedEx is a shining example of the concept of incrementalism at work. The organization had the vision to see an opportunity when others did not, and it proceeded to create a niche where one previously had not existed. FedEx utilized innovation to drive a series of small growth steps executed consistently over time. If one were to view these individual steps purely in isolation, they certainly would not appear significant. However, when you add up the daily sustained effort of these steps over time, you can see that the ensuing momentum built from its process from 1973 to today has resulted in massive success.

The myth about momentum is that many people equate momentum with luck. Others don't create momentum because they never try for fear that they don't have what it takes to achieve their goals. The reality is our goals aren't too high, rather our self-confidence is too low. Teams and organizations that consistently manufacture momentum play and compete at a higher level. Others don't create momentum because they believe it involves struggle and imposing your will on a task or on prospects. Fear of challenge, feeling overwhelmed, and lacking proper motivation also can prevent people from creating their own momentum.

Getting in the habit of manufacturing momentum is not just an athletic or business skill, it is a life skill. Nothing works unless you do, and nothing around you will get better until you do. Take targeted appropriate action even if it must be small actions. The Japanese concept of *Kaizen* involves the theory that small daily improvements eventually result in huge advantages. How? As in the case of FedEx, they add up over time, or in other words . . . through momentum.

You don't have to be a major corporation like FedEx to manufacture momentum. You just have to get started. Dream big, start small, act now.

Coaching Points

- How are you manufacturing momentum in your business?

- Rate your ability to focus in the present moment on a scale of 1-10 (1=low, 10=high).

- Are your goals top of mind? How can you keep them there?

- How would your co-workers, competitors, and clients rate your level of consistency?

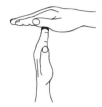

TIME OUT
MOMENTUM MAKERS

1. **Motion:** Create motion because motion leads to action.

2. **Game On:** Turn your tasks into a game, keep score and compete with yourself. If the task is unpleasant, turning it into a game can make it fun.

3. **Apply a coat of finish:** Finish what you have started, and make it a point to finish something to completion each day. Finishing feels good and brings about closure and a sense of accomplishment, not to mention forward progress. Furthermore, be sure to celebrate the finish because it is a small win for you.

4. **W.I.N.:** Make sure you are engaging in the most important activities. Don't confuse activity with productivity. Focus on What's Important Now (W.I.N.), and win the day!

5. **NBA:** When you've completed the most important tasks or when things go wrong, focus on the Next Best Action (NBA). What could and should you be doing next to propel yourself forward?

6. **Slow Down to Speed Up:** Sometimes we need to know when to call time out. The ability to take a break in order to rest, recover, and recharge will not slow your momentum, rather it is the secret to maintaining and sustaining it. Peak performers listen to their bodies and minds and consequently know when to strategically schedule breaks or taper down their training in order to continue to grow and achieve great results.

Chapter 22

The Underdog Advantage:
Competing When You're Not Number One

What you lack in talent can be made up with desire,
hustle and giving 110 percent all the time.
Don Zimmer, Major league baseball manager

As a recruiter, I always had an affinity for recruiting some "statistically smaller" players. Why? Quite simply, I liked the fact that they played with an additional chip on their shoulder. It's the right kind of chip though, not the typical negative-attitude one but rather the feeling that they have something to prove. They knew that given their stature they had to do the little extras to compete and stand out. These are the same little extras that the athlete who looks good on paper, 6 feet tall and 200 pounds, often will not do. These positive characteristics are the very things that don't get noticed by many recruiters because the athlete didn't fit the mold, the physical prototype, for a player at his position.

It is my belief that these little extras are what separate individuals or teams with similar talent. The ones willing to go the extra mile usually win. Over the years I found that many opponents overlooked and underestimated these players on my roster for similar reasons. As a result, the advantage went to the underdog. Simply put, in sport and business you can measure height, weight, and speed but you can't measure heart and mental toughness.

By the time these athletes reached college, they were used to the perception and embraced proving the critics wrong. This is not uncommon; underdogs are often exposed to more adversity. And the beauty of this is that adversity is an opportunity to develop resilience and create battle-tested confidence. See Figure 7 for the traits of an underdog.

Five Traits of the Underdog

1. *No fear.* Through superior preparation underdogs possess a quiet or subtle confidence. Unfavorable odds do not matter to underdogs because they draw faith and trust from knowing they have prepared to the best of their abilities. Having the understanding that every top dog was once an underdog enables the underdog to put a proper perspective on the competition.

2. *Self-Awareness.* Underdogs know themselves even better than they know their opponents. They succeed because they know precisely who they are and as importantly, who they aren't. Successful underdogs are comfortable in their own skin and don't try to be something they aren't.

3. *Creativity through Strategy.* Accentuate strengths, minimize weaknesses, and above all else differentiate yourself in a creative way to manufacture a competitive advantage. Underdog teams succeed because they have the right people in the right roles with the right goals for the right reasons.

4. *Opportunity.* Underdogs have their eyes open to identify a small window of opportunity and turn it into a gaping hole.

5. *Execution and Maximum Effort.* Underdogs stay the course, sustaining their effort and working their process to perfection.

Figure 7

Sometimes being the proverbial top dog is actually a disadvantage. These athletes are often accustomed to being the best on their team, in their department, at their level on the corporate hierarchy. When they move up to the next level, virtually everyone is comparable, and this culture shock can present an unfamiliar obstacle. On the other hand, this is an obstacle the underdog has literally had a lifetime of experience navigating.

The underdog advantage is what I call a confluence of talent, perseverance, and work capacity. You often hear coaches and leaders speak of the "it factor" when referencing a certain team member. The underdog advantage or this confluence is the "it factor" certain athletes possess.

As a coach of several underdog teams, I always tried to impress upon my players that outmanned does not mean outmatched. In sports you may see teams that lack size or depth yet make up for it with tenacity. In business you may see organizations that lack the financial or human resources of their competition yet are able to compete and win consistently. If you are not sold on the underdog advantage and believe resources are indeed everything, look no further than the New York Yankees with their all-star roster and enormous payroll. Yet they have not won the World Series with any more regularity in the past 20 years than the small market teams with only a fraction of the Yankees' resources. Contrast this with the NFL's New England Patriots whose payroll places it in the bottom 25 percent of the league yet has been the most successful team of the 21st century.

One of the underdog advantages is the heightened level of focus and concentration that results from a team knowing it has little or no margin for error in a game. We've all heard the expression in sports that a team played poorly and still won. That usually can be attributed to the fact that it was the heavy favorite, the more talented team, and consequently had a wide margin for error. Knowing it enjoyed this margin contributed to a lack of collective focus. That's something underdogs need not worry about.

Why is concentration and full effort important? It is one of the little things that can separate a champion from a runner-up. I always had a rule in practice, play to the whistle. Don't stop playing when things go wrong or when you think the play is over, keep playing hard until you hear a whistle. This rule may seem obvious or a ridiculous oversimplification, but trust me, coaches wouldn't have to coach this if it weren't a common problem. Case in point, in the 2011 BCS Football National Championship Game, the University of Oregon didn't play to the whistle on Auburn University's game-winning drive. Auburn running back Michael Dyer took a handoff from quarterback Cam Newton on a sweep play to the right. He appeared to be tackled by an Oregon defender after a small gain, and the Oregon defense literally stopped playing. However the referee never whistled the play dead. In reality, what happened was that Dyer rolled over the Oregon player and his knee never touched the ground, enabling him to keep his feet, bounce back up, and continue running down the right sideline for a massive gain of 37 yards. A lack of concentration by Oregon's defense allowed this play to set up the game-winning, last-second field goal, enabling Auburn to upset Oregon by a score of 22-19. This sort of momentary lapse of engagement happens every day in corporate America. Whether it is in business or a championship game, not playing to the whistle will get you beat and leave you wondering what might have been.

At the end of the 2002 season my St. Andrews College team faced a technically superior Mercyhurst College squad. It was ranked higher in the national polls and the media favored it by almost two goals, despite the fact that we had home field advantage. In the history of the rivalry between the two teams, St. Andrews had only beaten Mercyhurst once. To add to the pressure, the winner of the game advanced to the NCAA Final Four; the loser went home. During the week leading up to the game, my first concern was to make sure our players saw the game through the proper perspective. Instead of focusing on the history between the two teams or the fact that we did not match up particularly well, I wanted them to keep their eyes focused on the positives of the opportunity before them.

After reviewing film of Mercyhurst's games and analyzing our scouting reports, we came to the conclusion that we did not match up well in several key areas, particularly defensively against its potent attack. Our one advantage would be how we could match up in the midfield, provided we were successful in keeping the ball out of their attackmens' hands. We devised a game plan to limit Mercyhurst's ability to generate offense through its primary goal scorers. As a result, we were able to exploit weaknesses in its midfield play while also playing to our strength as an highly athletic group on offense who could score well in transition.

We had won five one-goal games and had several in dramatic come-from-behind situations, so I trusted that my players' perseverance and capacity for work wouldn't be an issue. I also felt they knew that with no margin for error focus and concentration would be at a premium. We had a mature squad, and it held true to form. After creating a turnover in the midfield, we marched the length of the field and scored a late transition goal to take the lead. The irony of the situation is that Mercyhurst was able to have a sustained possession and initiate offense through their very talented attackmen during the final two minutes of the game. Our defense and exceptional goaltender rose to the occasion, getting us several much-needed stops that allowed us to control the ball and kill the clock. The win was all heart and mental toughness . . . outmanned but not outmatched.

When I asked the players in our postgame team meeting what they saw as the keys to the victory, they indicated the freedom to go out and just play hard. Nobody expected them to win except the people in the locker room, and it turns out those are the only opinions that every really matter. They were in fact quite loose during the game, to the point of joking around with me to lighten my mood at various points in the huddle. Chalk up another lesson for the coach to learn from.

Like my 2002 St. Andrews team, all underdogs truly do enjoy the advantage of lowered public expectations. They can revel in the ability to play looser due to a lack of others' expectations. The pressure is on the heavily favored team or in the case of business, the industry leader. With that looseness, underdogs have a certain freedom and creativity that can be tapped into to enhance performance. While they can indeed enjoy this looseness, do not mistake the lowered public expectations to mean lowered personal expectations. Underdogs believe in themselves even when no one else does.

Intense self-belief is one of the key reasons why winners win consistently and specifically why underdogs win. The ability to stay true to your process, to work your process with faith and conviction often in the face of adversity, will determine your trajectory. This truth spans all industries whether your process is executing a game plan on the football field or executing the launch of a new product in the marketplace.

Underdogs in any field approach competition with a unique perspective. It is usually a perspective of self-awareness and internal focus. They are aware of their strengths, weaknesses, and unique competitive advantages. To understand the advantage of the underdog and how to tap into it, you must first understand what constitutes an underdog. Underdogs are teams, companies, individuals, and brands that are operating at a perceived competitive disadvantage in their respective industry.

I will frame this definition in a manner that will resonate with virtually anyone. For example, unless you are Nike, in the sneaker industry you are an underdog. Unless you are Google in the world of internet search engines, you are an underdog. While these dominant brands may have an overwhelming market share and enjoy a competitive advantage when it comes to financial resources, these advantages do not mean other companies in the industry cannot compete. Google got its start from humble beginnings, and Nike is the ultimate story of rising up from humble beginnings to international prominence. The original Nike waffle sole sneaker was literally made with a waffle iron in one of the founder's basements and sold out of the trunk of his car at regional track meets in the Pacific Northwest. When you trace the history of top dogs in virtually any industry, you will find underdog roots.

Necessity and adversity can be your best friends when you are faced with an underdog situation. Necessity and adversity can only have this effect if they are met with a willingness to change on your behalf.

Maximum sustained effort enables underdogs to consistently place themselves in the best position to be successful because when opportunity knocks, they are exceptionally well positioned to meet it. So much of life is about how we show up for situations and opportunities when they arise. Sometimes this may manifest itself in terms of effort. Consider the underdog athlete, team, or sales professional who shows up for the game or the big appointment feeling well less than 100 percent, say 80 percent. Its competitor, the "top dog," shows up feeling right at 100 percent but puts forth less than its best effort, performing at only 70 percent. If the underdog gives maximum effort, in other words gives 100 percent of the 80 percent it's got to operate with, it has a strong chance of winning. It can be argued in the case of Oregon vs. Auburn, the Oregon defensive players simply didn't sustain their effort. Opportunity knocked for Auburn, and it was indeed well positioned to meet it.

Coaching Points

- What can you do to help your people "play loose"?
- What will facilitate your team's heightened level of concentration and focus?
- How are you outmanned yet not outmatched in your business? Describe your advantage.

Chapter 23

Visualize Victory

It has to be a mentality before it's ever a reality.

John Brubaker, Performance consultant and author

On game day the final activity or closing ritual of my team's pregame warm-ups was always a shooting drill. Not just any shooting drill, rather one where every player experienced scoring a goal. We would run what I called the "game winning goal drill" on an empty net from close range, guaranteeing a positive outcome every shot. Standing at point blank range allowed my athletes to shoot the ball powerfully, accurately, and effectively. This drill is more than merely a closing ritual; it is designed to have every player visualize, experience, and feel success immediately prior to the start of the game. As a result, a positive feeling would carry over to the start of the game.

Imagine, for a moment, that we're able to approach all our personal and professional challenges with the same confidence and ability to visualize victory. The results would be phenomenal. Unfortunately, that is usually not the case. We know we ought to have a clear vision and the confidence to attack challenges head on but we oftentimes fall short or sabotage our own approach to the "game winning goals" in our lives for a variety of reasons.

Vision and desire are worthless without a willingness to pay the price for what you envision. Unlike the retail environment, you cannot purchase success on credit or layaway. The price is high, and the terms of purchase dictate that it be paid upfront with sweat equity and hard work prior to delivery. With that in mind, the first question I ask clients is, What do you want? Based on your answer, now. . . . What you are willing to earn?

The biggest gap for people is the gap between knowledge and practice. I call this the performance gap. Many people have an idea of the sort of "championship" they want: The student who wants to make Dean's list, the athlete who wants to be an All-American, the salesperson who wants to make President's Club, the actor who wants to win an Oscar. But do they have the drive, habits, and characteristics to transform dreams into reality? It all starts with an idea; however, the best ideas are useless without a vision and a plan to turn ideas into action, action into performance, and performance into championship caliber results.

"It has to be a mentality before it's ever a reality."

Champions approach each day with a performance mind-set. Champions in any industry—whether it be sports, business, or entertainment—have an "expect to win" attitude. They create a vision of success in their minds and more importantly employ laser-sharp focus on the process of making their vision a reality. The subconscious mind holds tremendous power and cannot tell the difference between reality and visualization, it simply responds to the thoughts we feed it. It is often said the best leaders are "visionary." It is no coincidence that the term "vision" is part of the description of their leadership style.

The concept of a performance mind-set is not just motivational mumbo jumbo; it is legitimately grounded in science and cognitive psychology. The reticular activating system or RAS is an area of the back of the brain near the spinal cord. In layman's terms this area of the brain contains the neural circuitry that determines what you see, think, feel, and hear. Perhaps more importantly, it also determines what you aren't going to see as well. You can think of the RAS as a filtration device for your brain. It is essentially an automatic mechanism that brings relevant stimuli and information in both your conscious and subconscious mind to your attention.

You can assist this filtration system by making adjustments to not only the way you work but also the way you think. The RAS is proof that what you think about you bring about. So, if you want to change your results, change your vision. Put into your mind that which you want to happen and remove from it the things you don't. Much like the exercise I shared with you of my players seeing themselves each score the game-winning goal. We wanted to put that vision in their heads during pregame and take out visions of self-doubt.

You cannot rely simply on the vision inside your head; to sustain your internal vision you need to supplement it by creating that same vision in your environment. By redesigning your work environment to align with your vision, you are enlisting the help of a powerful teammate. One of the reasons people have trouble sustaining a vision or making lasting changes is because in their attempt to change themselves and their mind-set they neglected to change the environment around them. Quite simply, you are trying to train your eyes to see success—to see opportunities that help you reach your vision. Your environment can be either a great facilitator or a great debilitator of your performance.

Developing a performance mind-set involves transforming your mind-set. Most people go through life living in particular circumstances, and the environment around them contains hurdles and obstacles that need to be overcome. Peak performers make an intentional decision to design their environment to be a setting that helps ensure their success.

By surrounding yourself with people, objects, and visual reminders that support and challenge you in a positive way, the odds of sustaining the vision and achieving victory increase dramatically.

To be effective, vision must be married to execution. The best teams I have coached not only possessed a unified vision of success, they also married it to execution. They walked the walk, understanding that success involves weighing opportunity cost. To them the opportunity to achieve greatness by far outweighed the cost of missing out on a few momentary pleasures. While their classmates chugged beer, they chugged protein shakes. While their roommates slept in, they awoke for 6 a.m. weight training. While their friends were on the beach at spring break, they were on the field running. Most teams and individuals fall short in these areas because they are not willing to make the investment of those daily deposits of hard work that accrue interest and can be withdrawn later when opportunity knocks.

Work habits dictate future success. I have seen several athletes over the years fall victim to their own success. Once they reached a certain level, such as All-American or All-Conference status, they thought they had arrived and had it all figured out. They stopped training as hard, cut back on off-season practice and preparations, and didn't put the same effort into studying film and scouting reports. Yet, when they were called on it, they were convinced they would achieve the same or better results in the upcoming season. Suffice it to say, they did not. The reason was simple. Their vision was no longer married to execution. Vision without execution is delusion.

In my consulting work, I sometimes see similar situations. I'm often approached by elite athletes and executives seeking peak performance coaching in order to regain that elite status they once enjoyed and somehow lost. The first thing I examine is their vision, figuratively speaking. What is their vision for success, and how do they define success? Then we will delve into their current process (assuming there is one).

Nine times out of ten this is the culprit; their process is not congruent with their vision. They are expecting to win in the sport of business without performing the right training, preparation, and conditioning. Superior results are the result of superior efforts. The principles don't change just because the environment does.

Any athlete or executive who wants to perform at his or her peak in the workplace needs to be physically and mentally at their peak. If you don't think like a champion and behave like a champion, you cannot become a champion. A helpful exercise I put my players through and that I now use with leaders and their teams is self-assessment. Many of my players knew it as the self-assessment of the perfect lacrosse player. For business professionals I have them replace the term "lacrosse player" with their job title. I ask them to list the mission critical activities and habits of someone who excels in that position. In other words, I am asking them to get clear on their vision of what excellence looks like in their role.

The exercise becomes their north star to a large extent. Vision with self-assessment enables them, with absolute clarity, to prove themselves to themselves. In my business we say over and over again that clarity facilitates optimal performance, whether it is the performance of an individual or a team. The main thing is the clarity. The mental aspect of success is even more important than the physical activities. Excellence in being, which starts with the vision in your mind, has greater power than mere excellence in doing.

Great leaders have great vision. It is a vision for their personal performance and the performance of their team. They inspire a greater effort and see the people in their organizations not for what they currently are but rather for what they can become. Part of inspiring this vision in their team is their living the vision as the example the team gets to see on a daily basis.

In addition to vision by example, I often felt the need to schedule specific vision meetings with my teams. It might take place the day after a loss, sometimes during a lull in the schedule, and often in the off-season when the light at the end of the tunnel seemed far away. The "vision meeting" as I called it became more of a vision conversation with team members, discussing the specific value and meaning of our collective vision to them. For example, our primary vision was often to focus on getting a little better every day. What that looks like to each player would vary greatly. The conversation often took on a life of its own with players volunteering their own recommendations on how we could best work to bring our vision to life through our daily actions. Over the course of a year or a season, these vision conversations became the vital link in keeping our vision top of mind, alive, and well.

The best brands in the world deliver a marketing and branding message that keeps their value top of mind to the consumer. For example, the marketing industry often refers to the "swooshification" of the sports apparel industry because of Nike's world-class branding, marketing, and advertising campaigns. Quite simply, the Nike swoosh is found practically everywhere you look. I wanted our team vision to have the same effect on each player on our roster. Unless we were advertising and creating a personalized call to action of the vision for each player, we could not expect them to keep it top of mind on their own. Our version of swooshifying our environment was to place personal vision boards in each player's locker, print them on t-shirts, have vision statements sent via campus mail, email, and snail mail on a consistent basis, and frame and display the team's collective vision board in the locker room.

Leaders in business can take this same process of vision building out of the locker room and into the board room. The work environment is actually a great starting point for building the vision of the team. The vision of victory for your team will be very personal and can differ greatly because every organization is unique. Every organization's definition of winning is unique as well. What is not different or unique are the attributes that define a winner and lie at the center of championship-caliber performance. This begs the questions of what does it take to become a champion and what do experts deem to be the most important qualities at the heart of a champion?

In 1999, Dr. Shari Kuchenbecker, a psychologist at Loyola Marymount University, performed a research study to determine the top characteristics for success in sports. She survey 658 coaches from 43 different sports, asking them to "describe an athlete who is a real winner" by selecting five attributes from a list of 64 physical and 64 psychological characteristics. The results indicated that the overwhelming majority of the coaches described "a real winner" by psychological attributes rather than physical.

The top five attributes selected were:

1. Loves to play the game (43%)

2. Positive Attitude (33%)

3. Coachable (30%)

4. Self-Motivated (27%)

5. Team Player (26%)

Interestingly, the first physical characteristic, "natural athlete," didn't appear on the list until number 19 and was selected by only 11 percent of the coaches surveyed. What does this tell us? (Beyond the fact that Yogi Berra wasn't far off in his statement that 90 percent of the game is half mental.) I believe it reveals you can apply the same attributes to other facets of your life to achieve success and reach your goals. You could survey CEOs and replace the word "athlete" with "businessperson" and the same attributes would rise to the top. Similarly, if you surveyed human resource directors and inserted the word "candidate" in place of "athlete," I bet almost identical results would follow.

It stands to reason that in business if we want to be successful and bring out the best in our people, we need to develop ways to encourage these five specific psychological attributes. To take it a step further, I would add that we also need to be seeking these habits in prospective recruits during the hiring process. There is no such thing as an overnight success, and performance is preceded by passion, attitude, and motivation. Cultivating these five attributes is something you can begin incorporating immediately into pursuit of your own personal championship.

Coaching Points
- What do you want, and what you are willing to earn?
- What thoughts and images do you need to put into your mind to support your vision internally?
- What do you need to remove?
- List three ways you can redesign your work environment to align it with your vision?

Part VII

OVERTIME

Chapter 24

Postgame Analysis

Success in the knowledge economy comes to those who know themselves – their strengths, their values, and how they best perform.

Peter Drucker, Management consultant and author

There are very few things more important in maintaining forward progress than a team's mind-set postgame. Whether after a win or a loss, the players' response to the event and their mind-set moving forward into the next week is of paramount importance. As a leader, you want them to hurt for a while after a loss but then put the loss behind them and move forward toward the next practice and next game. While many coaches agree it is important for players to take it personally when they lose and to learn from defeat, I have found very few coaches have an actual process for helping their team members reflect on and analyze their performance both collectively and individually. Without having a process or system in place to help the team learn from mistakes and apply those valuable lessons in their next performance, you cannot foster healthy team chemistry in the locker room, and you certainly can't ensure players won't make the same mistakes again.

The same can be said for managers, employees, and team chemistry in the corporate locker room. Take the financial services industry, for example. Financial advisors are corporate athletes in the truest sense. Like professional athletes, they control their schedules, training, goals, and productivity, and, most importantly, are responsible for their own results. The success of an advisor is measured on a scoreboard of sorts, assets under management. With this in mind, it is in the best interest of each firm's managing director and its advisors to engage in postgame analysis. As a leader, do you want to leave how your employees process a meeting up to chance or should you help them focus on the valuable takeaways they can gain from every performance?

What do you think about after a client meeting? Do you internalize the outcome, take a "no" too personally, and beat yourself up over what you wish you had said or done differently? Or without much analysis do you simply move on to the next appointment or task on your daily agenda?

If your answer fell on one extreme or the other, it is problematic on several levels. Not obsessing about a negative outcome is healthy, but if you do not engage in any analysis, you have missed a great opportunity for improvement by learning from your mistakes. Every meeting affords you an opportunity to learn more about yourself, your clients and prospects, the market, the business, and life in general.

Two mission-critical activities for financial advisors are looking out for the client's best interests and meeting with prospects for new business development opportunities. While these are clearly two high-priority areas, a third key to victory is making the investment in analyzing your interactions with clients and prospects. You analyze the performance of your client's investment portfolio and adjust the allocation of assets in order to make improvements. Why not think of your personal performance as a stock portfolio and do the same with these assets you call a career. After all, you've clearly invested heavily in it, and your future is riding on its performance. This investment of time has the ability to pay major dividends when performed effectively.

When you apply what you learn, you increase your chances for success.

To say most financial advisors tend to be competitive, type-A personalities would be an understatement. While this inner drive and competitive spirit can certainly facilitate success, at the same time, when channeled in the wrong direction, it can be an advisor's greatest hindrance. It is often said that our greatest strength is also our greatest weakness. This is definitely true with both athletes and executives.

Like a hitter in baseball, a business professional is going to experience more strikes and outs than hits and home runs when it comes to new business development. It is a game of numbers, a contact sport if you will. The more contacts you make with qualified prospects, the more opportunities to close new business exist. While this may be true, there are also steps you can take to increase your winning percentage. Professional basketball players often enlist the assistance of a shooting coach to analyze their shot and improve their mechanics. Shooting percentage was a statistic I always insisted my players pay careful attention to. To emphasize the fact that quality shots held greater value (and potential return) than the quantity of shots taken, I referred to shooting percentage as "net worth." You, too, can increase your net worth by analyzing your client meetings with the eight-question inventory shown in Figure 8.

During my coaching days, I performed a postgame analysis with my team after every game as a learning and teaching tool. A postgame review of performance helps make sure you are focused on the flawless execution of the right things as well as the little things, both individually and collectively as a team. (It is important to note that postgame analysis is conducted both in victory and in defeat.) After a loss, my assistant coach referred to this exercise as performing an autopsy. I prefer to think of it as preparing for the next victory. It is important to analyze performance in order to improve your preparation process because within every performance there are actually three performances:

1. The way you prepared to perform.
2. The way you actually went out and performed.
3. The way you wish you would have performed.

The goal is to create congruence between these three aspects of performance. In my work as a performance consultant, I have adapted this tool for business professionals and executives as the Client Meeting Analysis (Figure 8).

Client Meeting Analysis

1. *Rate your own level of mental and physical readiness for the meeting/appointment.* Do you engage in any performance rituals before meetings? How do you get mentally prepared to be a poised, confident communicator?

2. *Where did you perform well in the meeting?* Even if the meeting does not result in new business, you need to take stock of its successful elements and the strengths you displayed during the meeting. Put it in writing, and keep your postmeeting review sheets on file in a three-ring binder. Doing so will be a source of increased confidence for you as you enter the next meeting.

3. *Where could you have improved in the meeting?* Regardless of outcome, there are almost always one or two opportunities for improvement. There is sometimes a halo effect that surrounds victories where we convince ourselves that because we won it means we played well. In reality, more often than not that isn't the case. In

---

sports, there are ugly wins, and wins where you didn't so much earn the victory as have the other team beat itself. The same can be said for business.

4. *In what areas did your team perform well?* If you are presenting to a client with your team, it is important to have each member perform a postmeeting analysis. It will help each of you identify areas in your performance that may have previously been blind spots. It will also bring greater clarity to the meeting strategy for subsequent team presentations. The comparison of how each member of the team evaluates the collective performance will also be revealing.

5. *In what areas could your team have improved?* There should always be a sense of collective ownership of the quality of the meeting. By having team members isolate and identify areas needing improvement, you are facilitating this collective ownership. Answering this together also should serve to enhance the focus of the group for future meetings.

6. *What did the prospect or client do well?* In order to maximize the learning value of this postmeeting analysis, you need to be able to gain a better understanding of the person's strengths, goals, priorities, concerns, and objections. Where does the individual excel personally and professionally? What is his or her approach to working with an advisor? How would you describe his or her communication style and learning style?

7. *What did the prospect or client not do well?* What areas of her or his "fiscal fitness" does she or he struggle with, and how can you best help? Did the person communicate openly with you, or was she or he difficult to glean information from?

8. *Where did you make the greatest impact?* Having the self-awareness to answer this question effectively gives you insight into a strong jumping off point with the prospective client for follow-up meetings. It will also provide you with the ability to better play to your strengths in the future. If the meeting was a team presentation, take a moment and have each person reflect on the team members and the skills and strengths they exhibited. Where did they excel? Take this information, learn from it, and replicate it in future meetings.

Figure 8

In looking back over the stock market's performance in the new millennium, for a number of years a strong market elevated every advisor's performance. Consequently, it became difficult to filter out the good advisors from the truly great ones. Starting in 2008 many categorized the market conditions as poor; I prefer to think of this market as an opportunity for the great to rise to the occasion. With a downturn in any market, you have an opportunity to elevate and separate yourself from the competition. This is a window of opportunity for you to rise above conditions. Perseverance, a winning mind-set, and a commitment to excellence are the difference makers in your ability to stand out. While market conditions may be challenging, winners are at their best when conditions are not.

Whether you are a competitive athlete or a financial advisor, your mind-set has a significant impact on your level of success. It has been my experience that the best athletes I've coached are more concerned with losing than with winning. I am not referring to fear of failure, rather to the fact that winners expect to win and the fear of losing drives them to excel. The best of the best hold themselves to a higher standard. With that higher standard often comes a quest for constant self-improvement in order to gain or maintain that winning edge. I have consistently noticed that these same competitors tend to be the most highly coachable and introspective members of the team. The difference between a good performance and a great one or a one-goal loss and a close win comes down to the same things—little things. Little things win big games, and it is the little things that make a big difference in winning more business. What is usually the difference between scoring a goal and the goalie making a save? A slightly better shooting angle, a couple more steps closer to the goal, not staring down the target, quicker release, a fake, etc. All these are little things that when performed can enhance your chances for success and when neglected can cause you to beat yourself. By analyzing the seemingly little things in your client meetings, you can refine your game to gain or maintain your winning edge.

Chapter 25

The Final Score

When you win, say little; when you lose, say less.
Bill Belichick, Professional football coach

One of the great parallels between sports and business is the scoreboard by which you are measured at the end of the game or the end of the business day. In this book you have learned that success is facilitated by having a vision of your ultimate destination, without focusing solely on that vision. Your focus must instead be placed on the controllables; in other words focus on the process over the result. Being present in the moment one play or one sale at a time helps the proverbial scoreboard take care of itself.

As you begin to apply *The Coach Approach* principles in your personal and professional life, I want you to remember this: The only thing we have total control over in life is our effort and attitude. Athletes can't control the other team's or the officials' reactions; they can only control their response to a situation. Business is no different. Sales professionals can't control the buyer, their competitors, or the rules of engagement. They can only control their actions. Therefore success is not a destination but a direction, and that direction is forward not backward.

The two most important words to help you maintain forward progress are "Get Over." The phrase is appropriate both during times of adversity and times of excellence. When things go wrong, get over it and move forward. When things go well, get over yourself and move forward. I had a particular moment in my professional life that brought great clarity to this phrase and helped me shape this theory.

At my core I am a teacher and a coach. If you look up the definition of coach in a dictionary, it says that to teach is to coach and to coach is to teach. There are teachable moments all around you—in your professional life, as a businessperson, as a spouse, and as a parent. There's one such moment that stands out above all others for me.

In June 2002 less than two weeks after leading my team to the NCAA Final Four, I received an amazing phone call. My secretary, Millie, was this sweet Southern belle. She popped her head in my office and said, "Coaaaach Brubaykuuuh, you have a phone call from E-S-PEEEE-ANNN, would you like me to transfer it to y'all?" (In North Carolina "y'all" is singular, "all y'all" is plural.) Trying to act cool I said, "Sure, Millie. Thanks. That would be fine."

Meanwhile I was thinking, Wow this is great! This is how you know you've finally arrived. . . . ESPN calls YOU. My mind started racing, is it someone from *Sports Center, ESPN First Take,* ESPN Radio? Or maybe it's Roy Firestone, and he wants me to do one of those "Up Close" interviews. Then I immediately began wondering what questions the reporter was going to ask me. ("How did you take a team that never had a winning varsity season before your arrival and turn it into a national contender?" "Could you reflect on your road to the NCAA Final Four?") From time to time I'd let my assistant coaches field media requests to get them ready for being a head coach. So of course, my opportunistic assistant asked if this was one of those times. To which I responded, "No, not today. Even better, you get to watch how I handle the questions."

I thought I was being a mentor, always looking for those teachable moments. This was definitely one of them. We've arrived, hit the big time. . . . I'm ready!!

So I answer the call and much to my surprise the ESPN representative only called to ask one question that I will never forget. "Coach Brubaker, this is Richard from ESPN in Bristol Connecticut . . . . I am calling to see if you would like to renew your subscription to *ESPN The Magazine.* If you'll recall, last summer we sent all of the coaches in your department complimentary subscriptions, and they expire this month."

It was a teachable moment, alright. . . . for the teacher.

So I learned a big lesson that day. Get over yourself. You're not as good as you think, and you're certainly never as bad as the critics say you are.

Part of what helps you realize you're never as bad as they say and not quite as good as you think is the scoreboard on which you measure yourself. Warren Buffett refers to it as his internal scoreboard, "I keep an internal scoreboard. If I do something that others don't like but I feel good about, I'm happy. If others praise something I've done, but I'm not satisfied, I feel unhappy."

I utilize my success journal *3 by 5* as an internal scoreboard. It is my method of documenting successes. It allows me to literally close the book on past performances at the end of each day. I will only refer back to my journal when absolutely necessary. To keep a hungry and humble heart, I will also contemplate what one thing I could have done better each day and develop an action plan to do so moving forward into the next day. This strategy served me well as a coach, creating daily documentation of what our team did well, along with identifying a key area of improvement to focus on and devising a plan to do so.

The late Enzo Ferrari was the founder of Ferrari Motors. When his engineers showed him the prototype of the first Ferrari convertible, he sat down in the two-seater and examined it carefully. While he was quite impressed with how unique and innovative it was, he felt there was something just not quite right about the car. After a moment of silence, he found his key area of improvement, reached up, and ripped the rearview mirror off the windshield, saying, "When you drive a Ferrari, you never have to look behind you."

I don't think that philosophy is just about the performance of a Ferrari. Rather, it is a philosophy for peak performance in anything. Enzo Ferrari was right. What's behind you doesn't matter. Close the book on past performance, and either get over it or get over yourself. Take *The Coach Approach* and focus on the here and now. It's totally under your control.

Coaching Points

- How do you keep score on your internal scoreboard?
- How do you filter and eliminate the "crowd noise" from external sources?
- How are you seeking and celebrating successes with your team?
- What is your method of "removing the rearview mirror" to close the book on past performances?

Resources to Help You Implement
The Coach Approach

Now that you have completed reading *The Coach Approach*, you have an opportunity to incorporate *The Coach Approach* game plan into your personal and professional life. To assist you in achieving game–changing results, we encourage you to utilize the resources below.

www.TheCoachApproachGamePlan.com

Audio programs to coach you on executing *The Coach Approach* game plan right away.

- *The Coach Approach* motivational tools and products
- *The Coach Approach Game Plan Workbook*
- Share *The Coach Approach* system with your team and organization
- Join *The Coach Approach* online community

www.CoachBru.com

An array of resources for enhancing individual and team performance are available at CoachBru.com, including audio programs, articles, podcasts, peak performance products, and Coach Bru's blog. Details on booking Coach Bru to bring *The Coach Approach* to your organization are here as are audio and Kindle versions of *The Coach Approach*.

Build a Coach Approach Organization or Team

- The best way to improve a team is by improving the individuals. Help each of the members of your team or company become a *Coach Approach* style leader so that you can achieve the victory you so strongly desire. *The Coach Approach* is available at a special price on bulk orders for businesses, teams, colleges, and universities, as well as for nonprofits and civic groups. It makes a great gift to teach your people how they can bring out the best in themselves and those around them.

  Contact John Brubaker at 207-576-9853 or john@coachbru.com.

- To book a *Coach Approach* workshop for your team with Coach Bru, please contact The Sport of Business, LLC at www.CoachBru.com.

- Sign up for Coach Bru's e-newsletter at www.CoachBru.com

Coach Bru .com
JOHN BRUBAKER

J ohn Brubaker is a renowned performance consultant, speaker, and author. John teaches audiences how to obtain better results in business with straightforward tools that turbocharge performance. From college athlete to three-time coach of the year, to analyst and personality for ESPN Radio and Fox Sports, to consultant and author, John Brubaker knows the keys to take your performance to the next level. John uses a multidisciplinary approach to help organizations and individuals develop their competitive edge.

John Brubaker brings nearly 20 years of experience in teambuilding, leadership development, and coaching to his work as a performance consultant, speaker, and author. He is a 1992 graduate of Fairleigh Dickinson University with a bachelor's degree in psychology. He also earned a master's degree in personnel psychology from FDU in 1993. Brubaker has completed his doctoral coursework in Sport Psychology at Temple University. For more information visit: www.coachbru.com.

Notes

The Coach Approach

_____

_____

_____

_____

_____

_____

_____

_____

_____

_____

_____

_____

_____

_____

_____

_____

_____

_____